MINUTE GUIDE TO
Compuserve

Phillip Reed

A Division of Macmillan Computer Publishing with a Prentice Hall Macmillan Company

201 West 103rd Street, Indianapolis, Indiana 46290 USA

©1995 Que® Corporation

All rights reserved. No part of this book shall be reproduced, stored in a retrieval system, or transmitted by any means, electronic, mechanical, photocopying, recording, or otherwise, without written permission from the publisher. No patent liability is assumed with respect to the use of the information contained herein. Although every precaution has been taken in the preparation of this book, the publisher and author assume no responsibility for errors or omissions. Neither is any liability assumed for damages resulting from the use of the information contained herein. For information, address Que Corporation, 201 West 103rd Street, Indianapolis, Indiana 46290.

International Standard Book Number: 1-56761-427-2
Library of Congress Catalog Card Number: 9470401

95   8 7 6 5 4 3

Interpretation of the printing code: the rightmost number of the first series of numbers is the year of the book's printing; the rightmost number of the second series of numbers is the number of the book's printing. For example, a printing code of 94-1 shows that the first printing of the book occurred in 1994.

Screen reproductions in this book were created by means of the program Collage Plus from Inner Media, Inc., Hollis, NH.

Printed in the United States of America

Publisher: Marie Butler-Knight
Managing Editor: Elizabeth Keaffaber
Acquisitions Manager: Barry Pruett
Product Development Manager: Faithe Wempen
Development Editor: Kelly Oliver
Manuscript Editor: San Dee Phillips
Cover Designer: Dan Armstrong
Designer: Barbara Webster
Indexer: Charlotte Clapp
Production Team: Gary Adair, Dan Caparo, Brad Chinn, Kim Cofer, Lisa Daugherty, Bront Davis, David Dean, Jennifer Eberhardt, Beth Rago, Bobbi Satterfield, C. Small, Carol Stamile, Karen Walsh, Robert Wolf

Special thanks to Christopher Denny for ensuring the technical accuraacy of this book.

Contents

1 Introducing CompuServe, 1
What Is CompuServe?, 1
What Is WinCIM?, 2
Understanding Modems and System Requirements, 3

2 Signing Up for CompuServe, 6
Going Through the Signup Process, 6
Getting Your User ID Number
and Password, 9

3 Getting Started in WinCIM, 12
Starting WinCIM, 12
Getting to Know the Desktop, 13
Connecting to CompuServe , 16
Disconnecting from CompuServe and Exiting WinCIM, 17

4 Using the Desktop Features to Navigate CompuServe, 19
Navigating CompuServe, 19
Using the Go Icon, 20
Using the Find and Favorite Places Icons, 21

5 Identifying the Cost of a Service, 25
The Meter Is Running, 25
Pricing Before You Spend, 28

6 Getting Help, 30
Answering WinCIM Questions, 30
Using WinCIM's Help System, 30
Getting Help Online, 33

7 Filing and Downloading Information, 36
Reversing the Flow, 36
Retrieving Files, 38

8 Editing and Printing a File with Notepad, 40
Using Notepad, 40
Getting to Know Notepad's Features, 41

Opening a Document, 41
Editing in Notepad, 43
Undoing Mistakes, 44
Setting Up and Printing Files
in Notepad, 45

9 Viewing News and Weather Reports, 47

Keeping Up-to-Date with CompuServe, 47
Viewing News Reports, 47
Viewing Weather Reports, 50
Looking at Weather Maps, 51

10 Using the Electronic Library, 54

Using CompuServe's Reference Sources, 54
Using the Electronic Encyclopedia, 55
Searching for Missing Persons, 57

11 Searching a Magazine Database, 61

Doing Research on CompuServe, 61
Using Magazine Database Plus (CIM), 62

12 Setting Up Your Address Book, 68

What Is the Address Book?, 68
Adding an Address to the Address Book, 69
Looking Up a Member's Address, 70
Copying Member Addresses to the Address Book, 71
Managing the Address Book, 72

13 Sending E-Mail, 75

What Is E-mail?, 75
CompuServe Mail Features, 75
Creating the Message, 76
Sending the Message, 81
Sending Mail from the Out-Basket, 81

14 Receiving Mail, 83

Using CompuServe's Mail System, 83
Getting Your Mail, 84
Reading Mail Offline, 85
Managing Your In-Basket
with the File It Button, 86
Automating Your Mail, 87

Contents

15 Sending Files, 89
Using the Send Files Option, 89
When to Send Files, 90
Getting Ready to Send a File, 91
Sending a File, 93

16 Receiving Files, 95
Moving Files from CompuServe into Your System, 95
Getting a File, 96
Finding and Moving a File, 98

17 Using the Internet, 101
Getting Ready for the Internet, 101
Sending E-Mail on the Internet, 102
Receiving E-Mail on the Internet, 104
The Internet Forum, 105

18 Online Shopping, 107
Shopping Unlimited, 107
Entering the Mall, 108
Using Merchant QuickSearch, 109
Choosing a Department and a Product, 110
Using Product QuickSearch, 112

19 Making Travel Plans, 114
Using EAASY SABRE (CIM), 114
Checking Fares, 117
Visiting the Itinerary Feature, 119

20 Using Forums, 121
Understanding Forums, 121
Forum Activities, 122
Searching a Forum for a Program, 124
Downloading a Forum File, 126

21 Joining Forums and Posting Messages, 128
Finding Your Forum, 128
Creating a Forum Message, 131

22 Financial Services, 134
Managing Your Money, 134
Checking Your Stocks, 135

Inputting Your Stocks, 135
Looking Up a Ticker Symbol, 136
Charting a Stock's Performance, 138
Getting a Stock Quote, 139
Personal and Business
Financial Services, 141

23 Customizing WinCIM, 142
Creating Your Own Work Environment, 142
Changing Preferences, 144

A Windows Basics, 147
Tell Me About Windows, 147
Starting Microsoft Windows, 147
Parts of a Windows Screen, 148
Using a Mouse, 149
Starting a Program, 150
Using Menus, 150
Navigating Dialog Boxes, 151
Switching Between Windows, 153
Controlling a Window, 153

B Working with Modems, 154
Failure to Connect with CompuServe, 154
Other Modem Related Problems, 156
Changing Baud Rates, 157

C The Cost of Services, 158
Two Payment Plans, 158
Standard Pricing Plan, 158
Alternative Pricing Plan, 159
CompuServe Product Categories, 159

D File Compression, 160
Setting Up PK204g.EXE, 160

Index 163

Introduction

CompuServe is a tool for the information age. Like any other took, it only becomes valuable when you know how to use it. That's the first purpose of this book, to explain the basics of this powerful online service that brings information not just to your front door, but right into you home.

There are, however, two other important benefits you can gain form reading this guide.

In its desire to offer something for everyone, CompuServe often seems a bit overwhelming. By following these lessons, you will get a taste of some specific ways CompuServe can help you do your job and enjoy your free time.

The final benefit to be listed here is really two inter-related things: time and money. Since many of the services cost the user extra for each minute online, the efficient CompuServe navigator will save both time and money.

With the above listed benefits, the reader and CompuServe explorer will discover many unexpected treasures along the way.

Conventions Used in This Book

Throughout this book, you will find four types of icons to help you quickly find important information:

Timesaver Tips offer ways to streamline your use of CompuServe. Often, this will also be a way to save money.

Plain English icons appear to define new terms.

Panic Button icons identify potential problems areas and how to solve them.

Go icons provide you with a quick reference word that takes you directly to a certain area of CompuServe.

Specific conventions in this book help you to easily find your way around CompuServe.

What you type   appears in bold, color type.

What you select   appears in color type.

On-screen text   appears bold.

Acknowledgments

A number of talented people assisted in the creation of this book. Special thanks to Kelly Oliver at Alpha Books, and Michelle Moran at CompuServe.

Lesson

Introducing CompuServe

In this lesson, you will learn about some of the things CompuServe can do for you. Also, you'll learn how to obtain the software to run CompuServe and which hardware you'll need to go online.

What Is CompuServe?

Maybe you're a student writing a paper about international politics. Perhaps you want to exchange e-mail (electronic mail) with friends across the country. Or maybe you're looking for the latest version of your favorite computer game. If you have any of these interests—or a hundred others—the world of CompuServe is extremely useful and endlessly fascinating.

CompuServe is an online information service that you access with your computer and a *modem*. When you connect to CompuServe, your computer becomes more powerful. Also, the CompuServe system enables you to find other people with similar interests and communicate with them electronically. To join CompuServe is to become part of a vast network that brings people together and provides information resources.

Modem An electronic device that sends and receives information across telephone lines. A modem is either *external* (a small box that sits next to your computer) or *internal* (a computer card that plugs into the motherboard of your PC).

Lesson 1

Here are just a few things CompuServe enables you to do:

- Read the most recent news and weather reports.
- Send electronic mail messages (e-mail) to other computer users.
- Search for articles from thousands of periodicals.
- Exchange information about your profession or interests.
- Search for and buy the lowest rates on airline tickets and hotel rooms.

CompuServe is continually being modified and enlarged. As you learn to use CompuServe, you will become better at tailoring this service to your individual needs.

What Is WinCIM?

WinCIM is the software that enables you to connect to CompuServe and use it. This book covers version 1.3 of WinCIM.

WinCIM WinCIM stands for CompuServe Information Manager for Windows. Like many Windows-based applications, WinCIM has a specific graphic style and is easier to use than its DOS-based counterpart (see Figure 1.1).

I Don't Do Windows! This book is for the reader who is familiar with the Windows environment. If you don't have much experience with Windows, turn to the Microsoft Windows Primer (Appendix A) at the back of this book for help.

Introducing CompuServe 3

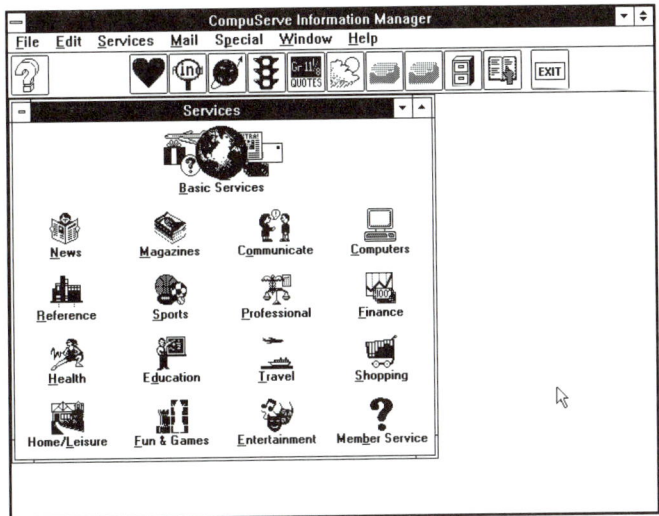

Figure 1.1 WinCIM resembles many Windows applications.

If you don't have the WinCIM software yet, you can obtain it by doing one of the following things:

- Call CompuServe (1-800-848-8990) and have them send you WinCIM .
- Buy WinCIM from a computer software store.
- Order WinCIM through a mail order house.

Once you obtain the software, you can install it on your computer's hard drive. (For installation instructions, refer to the inside front cover of this book.) Then, call CompuServe and sign up by providing a credit card number and supplying other details. (See Lesson 2 for more information on signing up.)

Understanding Modems and System Requirements

To access CompuServe with the WinCIM software you must have:

Lesson 1

- A hard drive with at least 4MB (megabytes) of disk space and a high-density floppy disk drive.
- At least 2MB of memory (RAM).
- An 80386 microprocessor or higher.
- A mouse (highly recommended).
- Microsoft Windows Version 3.1 or higher.
- An EGA (or better) monitor that is Windows-compatible.
- A modem. A *Hayes-compatible* modem is recommended.

> **Hayes-Compatible Modem** Any modem that has a standardized set of instructions developed by Hayes. Most modems fall into this category. Look on your modem or the box it came in for this specification. (More on this in Lessons 2 and 3 and Appendix B.)

Connecting to CompuServe requires no special knowledge of modems. By following the directions in Lesson 2, you should be able to connect to CompuServe and sign up to become a member.

Picking Your Payment Plan

Before you call to sign up, you should decide how you want to pay for CompuServe. There are two payment plans:

- **Standard Pricing Plan** CompuServe charges a monthly rate (currently $8.95) for unlimited use of the basic services. Among the features included in basic services are news, weather, sports, financial information, a reference library, and access to an electronic shopping mall. Also, you can send up to 60 three-page e-mail messages. CompuServe bills

Introducing CompuServe

you for extended services—special pay-as-you-go services—according to the *baud rate* of your modem (see Figure 1.2).

- **Alternative Pricing Plan**   Under this arrangement, CompuServe charges a $2.50 monthly membership support fee plus an hourly rate for your connect time. The hourly rate varies from $6.30 to $22.80 depending on the baud rate of your modem.

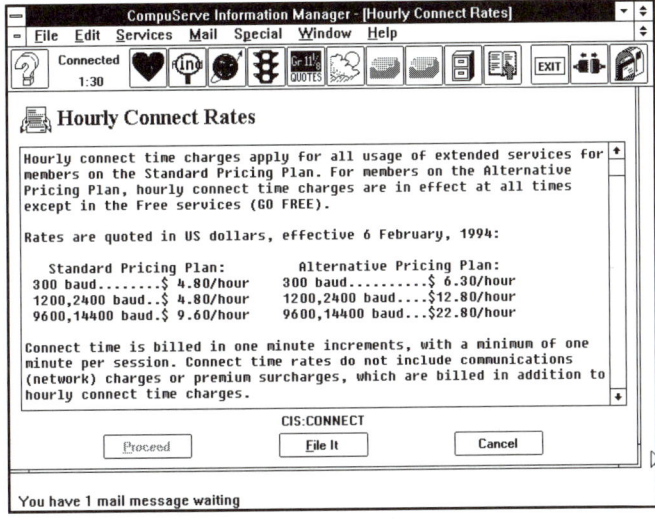

Figure 1.2   CompuServe bases your charges on the baud rate of your modem.

Baud Rate   The speed at which a modem transfers information. The higher the baud rate, the faster your computer can communicate with CompuServe. Common baud rates are 300, 1200, 2400, 9600, and 14400.

In this lesson, you learned about some of the features of CompuServe. You also learned where to buy the WinCIM software. In the next lesson, you will sign up for CompuServe.

Lesson

Signing Up for CompuServe

This lesson will take you through the signup process for CompuServe. You will receive your User ID number, password, and a local phone number to call when accessing the CompuServe network.

Going Through the Signup Process

CompuServe has designed a quick and easy signup process. You simply reply to questions on the screen, provide certain information, and you become a member. If a U.S. user encouters any problem signing up he or she can get help by calling 1-800-609-1674.

To go through the signup process, follow these steps:

1. From Program Manager, double-click the CompuServe group icon, and the CompuServe window appears.

2. Double-click the Membership Sign Up icon (see Figure 2.1). The Signup dialog box appears with copyright information.

3. Click Proceed. The Signup menu appears.

4. Click Sign up on the Signup menu. The Signup - Billing/Country dialog box opens (see Figure 2.2).

Signing Up for CompuServe 7

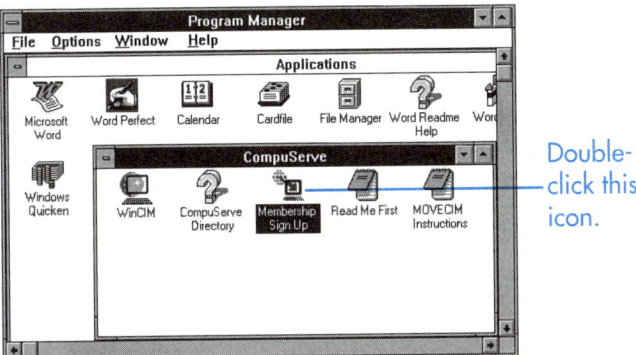

Figure 2.1 Begin the signup process by selecting the Membership Sign Up icon.

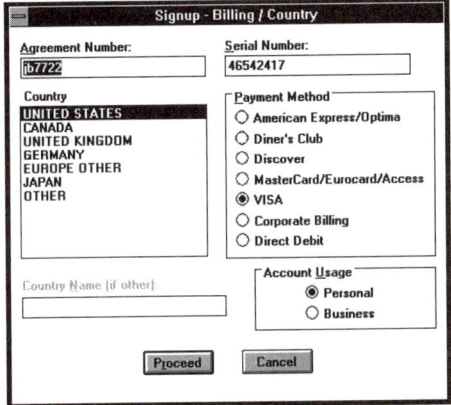

Figure 2.2 The Signup - Billing/Country dialog box.

5. Fill in the Agreement Number and Serial Number text boxes. These numbers are on the Important Operating Instructions card that comes with the software.

6. Choose the country and method of payment. Note that not all payment methods work for all countries.

Lesson 2

7. Click Proceed. The CIM - Signup dialog box appears. Enter your information and choose membership options. (Use your area code in the phone number.)

8. Click Proceed. The Signup - Executive Option dialog box appears offering an Executive Service.

9. (Optional) Click the Details button to read more about this service and possibly join.

10. Click No to decline or Yes to accept the Executive Service Option. The CompuServe Information Agreement Terms dialog box appears.

11. Read the information and then click Proceed. The Signup Phone Dial Type box dialog appears.

12. Click the option button for the correct description of the kind of phone you have.

13. Click Proceed. The Signup - Communications Port dialog box appears (see Figure 2.3).

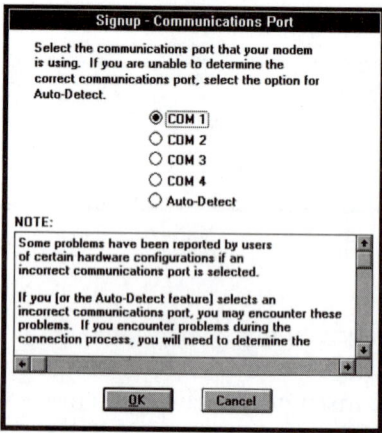

Figure 2.3 Choose the communications port your modem uses.

14. Click the option button for the *communications port* your modem uses.

Signing Up for CompuServe

Communications Port The port in the back of your system unit (generally called "COM port") that connects a peripheral to your computer. Computers have at least two COM ports: one for the mouse (usually COM1) and one for the modem (usually COM2).

COM Port Confusion Many computer users don't know which COM port their modem uses. Try COM2 first. If it doesn't work, you can use trial and error to find the modem's COM port. When you've found the correct setting, you'll hear your computer dialing a phone number at step 1 of the next section.

15. Click OK. A message appears, advising you that Signup is going to connect to CompuServe.

Getting Your User ID Number and Password

You are about to connect with CompuServe for the first time. This connection is only to exchange signup information with CompuServe. You will receive your User ID number and password; have pen and paper handy.

1. Click the Signup button. Your modem automatically dials an 800 number, and you connect to CompuServe. Eventually, a dialog box appears labeled **Welcome to CompuServe**.

No Connection If your modem fails to connect with CompuServe, try clicking the Signup button again. If you don't hear your modem dialing (it sounds like high-pitched beeps), check your COM port settings (see the previous section). If your modem dials and CompuServe answers, but the connection is lost, see Appendix B or call CompuServe Technical Support (1-800-848-8990).

Lesson 2

2. Review the agreement information in the box; then type Agree.

3. Click Proceed. You automatically disconnect from CompuServe, and the Signup - Account Information dialog box appears (see Figure 2.4).

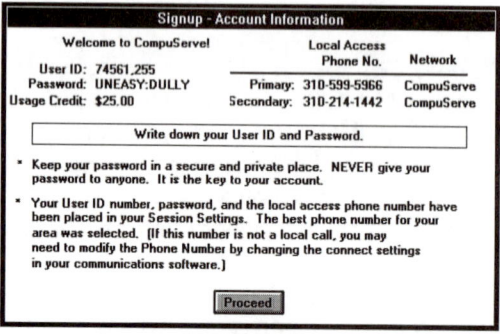

Figure 2.4 CompuServe provides your User ID number and password in this screen.

4. Write down your ID number and password. Put this information in a safe place for future reference.

5. Click Proceed. A second Signup Account dialog box appears.

6. Click the Finished button. The CIM - Signup dialog box asks you to confirm that you have accepted your ID number and password.

7. Click the OK button. The Personal Information dialog box appears.

8. Read the information, then click the Done button. You return to the CompuServe window.

9. (Optional) Double-click on the CompuServe window's Control-menu box to return to Program Manager.

Signing Up for CompuServe

Congratulations, you've now completed the signup process and have everything you need to connect to CompuServe. Rest assured that you won't have to go through this process again.

In this lesson, you learned how to sign up for CompuServe and you received your User ID number and password. In the next lesson, you will learn about the WinCIM desktop, and then connect to CompuServe.

Lesson 3

Getting Started in WinCIM

In this lesson, you will learn about the WinCIM desktop, and you will learn how to connect to and disconnect from CompuServe.

Starting WinCIM

Before you can start WinCIM, you need to make sure Windows is running. If you haven't started Windows yet, type **WIN** at the DOS prompt, and then press Enter. Windows will start; the Program Manager window should be on-screen.

To start the WinCIM program, follow these steps:

1. From the Program Manager window, double-click the CompuServe group icon. The CompuServe group window opens.

2. Double-click the WinCIM icon (shown in Figure 3.1). The program starts, and you see the WinCIM desktop.

When you start WinCIM, the Connect to CompuServe dialog box appears. For now, click the Continue button instead of the Connect button. (You'll learn how to connect later in the lesson.) There are many things you can do in WinCIM without using CompuServe; for example, you can search for help topics, read files you previously retrieved from CompuServe, or create an e-mail message.

Getting Started in WinCIM   13

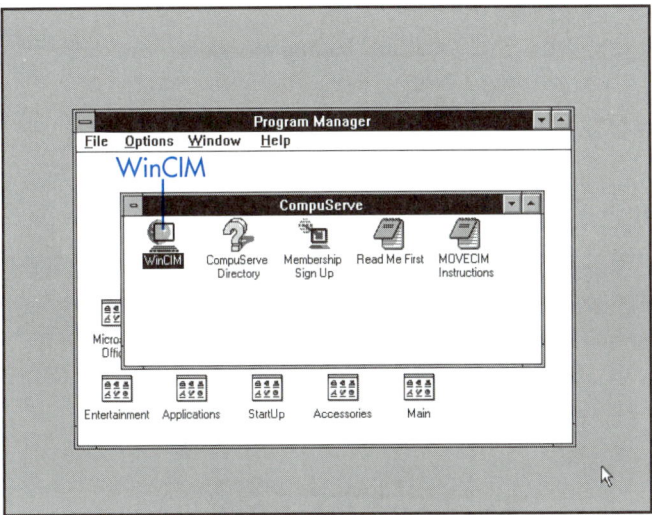

Figure 3.1 The WinCIM icon.

Is This CompuServe? Make sure you understand the difference between the software and the online service. The software (WinCIM) simply provides the means for retrieving data from the online service (CompuServe) and exchanging information with other CompuServe members. WinCIM is an *interface*, because it allows you to communicate, or interact, with the online service.

Getting to Know the Desktop

The *desktop* is WinCIM's main screen. It contains many elements (shown in Figure 3.2) you should become familiar with before you connect to CompuServe. It has many of the same features as most Windows-based programs, but it also has a few extras. The next few sections explain the parts of the WinCIM desktop.

Lesson 3

The Desktop The main screen you see when you first load WinCIM. From the desktop, you use pull-down menus, icons, windows, and dialog boxes to navigate CompuServe.

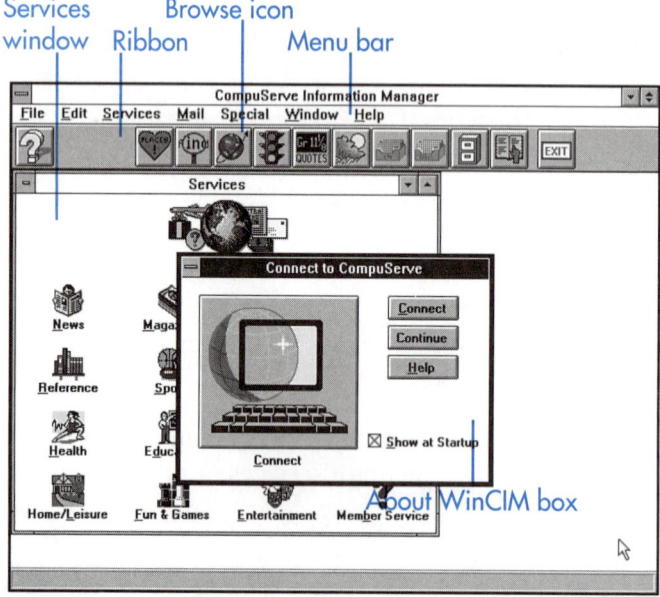

Figure 3.2 The WinCIM desktop.

Using WinCIM's Menu Bar

Toward the top of the screen, right under the title bar, is WinCIM's menu bar. To open a pull-down menu and select a command, click on the menu name. When the menu drops down, click on the command.

For example, to select an editing command, click on the word Edit in the menu bar, and then click on the command you want. You can also activate a menu by holding down the Alt key and pressing the underlined letter in the menu name.

Getting Started in WinCIM

If you open a menu and then decide you don't want to use it, just click anywhere else on the desktop, or press Esc.

Using the Ribbon

Below the menu bar is the Ribbon. It contains many *icons*: buttons that represent frequently used commands or features. To use the command or access the feature the icon represents, click on the icon. (See the inside back cover of this book for a list of the icons and their purposes.)

The Services Window

You can go to any of CompuServe's services by using the Services window. Select the category for the service you want to use by clicking the appropriate icon. For example, if you want to read the latest news stories, click the News icon.

When you click an icon, a Display Menu dialog box appears that contains a menu of services or other categories to select. You'll learn more about dialog boxes later.

> **Just Browsing** Sometimes, when you have many open dialog boxes, the Services window gets buried. You can see the Services window at any time by clicking the Browse icon on the Ribbon (shown in Figure 3.2).

If you want to close the Services window, double-click on its Control-menu box.

The Connect to CompuServe Dialog Box

The Connect to CompuServe dialog box appears when you start WinCIM. You can click the Connect button to connect to the CompuServe network, or you can click the Continue button to close the dialog box without going online. If you don't want this dialog box to appear every time you start WinCIM, click the Show at Startup check box to deselect it.

Connecting to CompuServe

You automatically connect to CompuServe, or "go *online*," when you click an icon in the Services window; when you select a command that uses information that's stored on the network; or when you send a file or e-mail message to another CompuServe member.

OnLine When you connect to the network, you are online. If you do not connect to the network, you are offline.

If you'd like to go online now—just to see what it's like—follow along with this example:

1. Click the Basic Services icon in the Services window. You automatically connect to the network and the CompuServe dialog box appears. (This is a Display Menu dialog box, but from now on I'll just refer to it as a dialog box.)

2. Double-click the Member Assistance item. The Member Service dialog box opens, with many categories to choose from (see Figure 3.3).

3. Go ahead and double-click on a topic to open a window with information on the topic.

4. When you're done reading the information, click the Cancel button to close the window.

5. Click the Cancel button in each dialog box until you return to the Services window.

Now, look at the Ribbon. Notice that it looks a little different than it did when you were offline. A new icon, the Disconnect icon, appears at the end of the Ribbon. Also, the word **Connected** appears in the space next to the Help icon. Notice that there is also a timer in that space. It keeps

Getting Started in WinCIM 17

track of how long you are connected to CompuServe. In this book, I'll call this space on the Ribbon the *status area*, to keep it separate from the icons on the Ribbon.

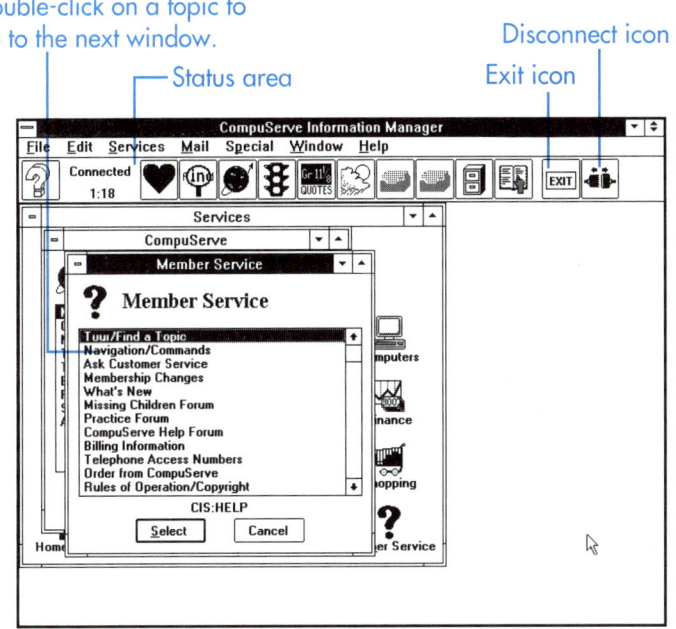

Figure 3.3 The desktop changes when you connect to CompuServe.

Disconnecting from CompuServe and Exiting WinCIM

When you finish using CompuServe, there are two different ways to disconnect. You can disconnect from CompuServe but keep WinCIM running, or you can disconnect from CompuServe and exit WinCIM all at once.

The fastest way to disconnect and/or exit is to click on either the Disconnect icon or the Exit icon (see Figure 3.3). Choose one of the following methods:

Lesson 3

- Click the Disconnect icon on the Ribbon. A box appears momentarily, letting you know that WinCIM is disconnecting you from CompuServe. You will no longer be online, but you can still use the WinCIM software.

- Click the Exit icon on the Ribbon. You disconnect, exit WinCIM, and return to Program Manager—all at once.

What Disconnect Icon? If you don't see a Disconnect icon on the Ribbon, that means you are not connected to CompuServe. The Disconnect icon only appears on the Ribbon when you are online. To exit WinCIM when you are offline, just click the Exit icon on the Ribbon.

In this lesson, you learned how to start and exit WinCIM, about the WinCIM desktop, and how to connect to and disconnect from CompuServe. In the next lesson, you'll learn how to find a specific service.

Lesson 4

Using the Desktop Features to Navigate CompuServe

In this lesson, you will learn how to use WinCIM desktop features to find your way around CompuServe.

Navigating CompuServe

The WinCIM desktop provides several ways to accomplish tasks and navigate CompuServe's services. These include:

- Accessing commands via the menu bar.
- Clicking icons in the Ribbon.
- Selecting the Go icon and typing the service name in the dialog box that appears.
- Using the Find icon to search for services you use most often.
- Adding the services you use most often to your Favorite Places list.

> **Services** The services in CompuServe are the different areas or features it provides. The services can be thought of as departments in a store. The most popular features are listed in the Services window.

Lesson 4

In the beginning, you can use the pull-down menus and the icons on the Ribbon. (The menu bar and the Ribbon were covered in Lesson 3.) As you become familiar with CompuServe, you will know where you want to go, and you won't need the menus to help you. If you know which service you need, you can use the Go icon to go straight to the service and save time. If you aren't sure which service you need, you can click the Find icon to search for it.

Using the Go Icon

The Go icon on the Ribbon looks like a traffic light. When you click the Go icon, the Go dialog box appears, allowing you to enter a quick reference word in the Service text box. When you click OK or press Enter, you go straight to a specific area. Use this icon for bypassing in-between steps and going where you want quickly.

GO! Click the Go icon to go straight to a specific service.

Quick Reference Words Quick reference words take you straight to a specific service. You click the Go icon, then type the quick reference word and press Enter.

For example, the following steps show how to use the Go command.

1. Click the Go icon. The Go dialog box appears, as shown in Figure 4.1.

Using the Desktop Features to Navigate CompuServe 21

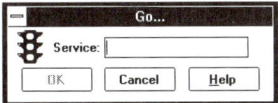

Figure 4.1 The Go dialog box.

2. Type the name of the service you would like to go to. For example, type Questions to reach Customer Service.

3. Click OK. You connect to CompuServe, and a new dialog box appears.

4. Click Cancel to return to the Services window.

> **Know the Command** Click the Go icon and type **Commands** to get additional information about navigating WinCIM. You can then see an index and list of quick reference words by selecting Quick Reference Words in the Navigation/Commands dialog box.

Using the Find and Favorite Places Icons

CompuServe is so vast you may not know where to look for what you need. To search for information on a subject, use the Find icon (see Figure 4.2). Use the Find feature like you use the index of a book; search for each service by subject. Once you locate a useful service, add it to your list of Favorite Places (as explained later in this lesson) so you can easily find the service the next time you want it.

Lesson 4

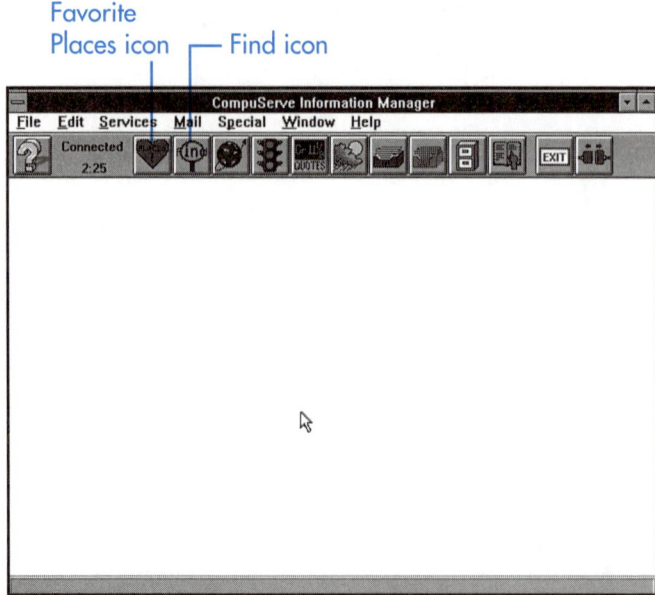

Figure 4.2 The Find and Favorite Places icons.

For example, let's say you're a movie buff and frequently want to read current film reviews. Starting from the Services window, follow these steps:

1. Click the Find icon on the Ribbon (see Figure 4.2). The Find dialog box appears.

2. Type **movies** and press Enter. The Search Results dialog box appears, listing subject headings about movies in the box on the left side (as shown in Figure 4.3).

3. Scroll down to Roger Ebert's Movie Reviews, and highlight it.

Lesson 5

Identifying the Cost of a Service

In this lesson, you will learn how to identify the cost of a service by using the Rates command.

The Meter Is Running

There are many features in CompuServe that you will want to use even though they carry an extra charge. These are the extended and premium services. You should make it a habit to check the rates on these services before using them.

You can find the cost of services in several ways:

- By looking at the code following the service title—which will be a $, a + (plus sign), or $E.

- By selecting Pricing Information from the service's menu.

- By using GO RATES.

- By turning to Appendix C of this book, "The Cost of Services."

Deciphering Costs

Trying to figure out the exact cost of services may confuse you. However, you can always get a listing of the most up-to-date charges by using the Rates command.

Lesson 5

GO RATES Use GO RATES to see a list of charges.

To see a list of the cost of charges, follow these steps:

1. Close any dialog boxes or windows on your screen so that only the Services window is showing.

2. Click the Go icon.

3. Type Rates in the dialog box and click OK. You connect to CompuServe, and the Current Rates dialog box appears.

4. Double-click the Hourly Connect Rates item. A chart appears, showing the cost of the extended services (see Figure 5.1).

5. Use the scroll bars to see all the information.

6. Click on Cancel to close the dialog box.

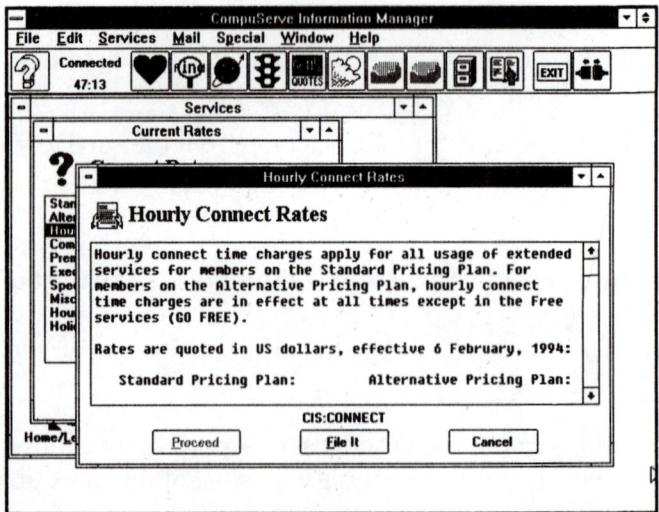

Figure 5.1 Hourly connect rates.

Identifying the Cost of a Service   27

Am I Being Charged for This? Remember, if you are on the Alternative Pricing Plan, you pay an hourly connect time fee at all times except when using the free services. For an explanation of the Standard and Alternative Pricing Plans, see Lesson.

The baud rate of your modem determines the hourly connect rate of extended services. Connect rates in increments of one minute determine your cost, so it's useful to determine the cost per minute. The 1200 and 2400 baud connect rate is $.08 a minute while the 9600 and 14400 baud connect rate is $.16 a minute.

Surcharges for Premium Services

Some services carry surcharges in addition to the hourly connect rates. This usually relates to the downloading of information. For example, it may cost you $1.50 to download a magazine article.

Download *Downloading* a file means to move a copy of it from another computer (in this case, CompuServe) to your computer. *Uploading* is the opposite. You move a copy of a file from your computer to another computer.

There is an optional membership tier in CompuServe called *Executive Services*. This is specialized and is beyond the scope of this book. If you need help with Executive Services, check the on-line Help system or the software documentation.

GO FREE For a user on the Alternative Plan, GO FREE will bring up a list of free services. Connect time charges and additional fees do not apply to these services.

Pricing Before You Spend

Another useful feature of the Rates command is the Premium Services window. This helps you calculate your costs ahead of time so you can avoid shock and outrage when your credit card bill arrives each month.

Let's say you are looking for a hard-to-find book. You decide to use the Books in Print service and want to know the cost of looking up a book. From the Current Rates dialog box (see steps earlier in this lesson), follow these steps:

1. Double-click the Premium Services option. The Premium Surcharges dialog box appears, listing CompuServe departments.

2. Double-click Reference. The Reference dialog box appears.

3. Double-click Books in Print. An Assistance window appears listing surcharges that are additions to the basic CompuServe connect rate.

4. Review the charges (see Figure 5.2).

5. (Optional) Click the File It button to store this information for future reference. For more information about the File It button, see Lesson 7.

An unsuccessful search costs $1 (see Figure 5.2). If you find and download information on a book, the total cost is $4: $2 for the search and $2 for downloading the entry.

> **Read Offline and Save Money**
> CompuServe provides an easy way to capture information and read it offline to avoid hourly connect rates. If a File It button appears, click it, then click the Save button. After disconnecting from the CompuServe network, you can retrieve the document from the Filing Cabinet and read it at your leisure. See Lesson 7 for more information about the File It button.

Identifying the Cost of a Service   29

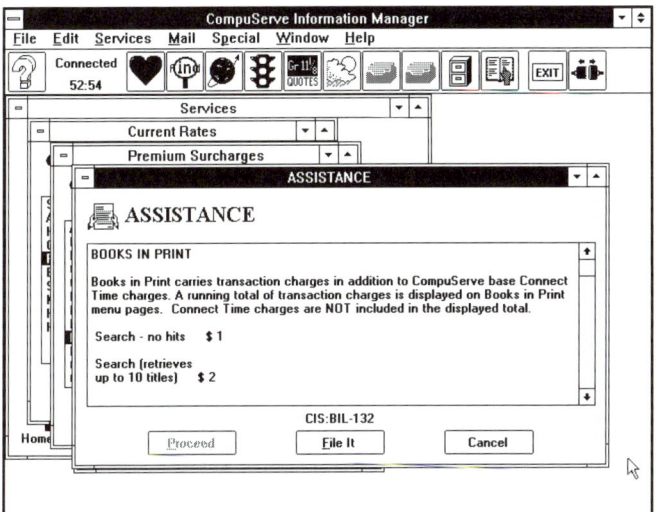

Figure 5.2 Pricing information on a premium service.

Finding More Ways to Save

There are several easy ways to save money while using CompuServe:

- Download information and read it offline (as explained in Lesson 7).

- Use practice forums to speed your use of extended services. Free practice forums are provided to increase your ability to use forums before you pay to use forums in extended services.

- Read the Specials (GO SPECIALS) for offers of credit or discounts.

- Plan every step you're going to take before entering extended or premium services. That way, you can avoid unnecessary connect time.

In this lesson, you learned how to find out what a service will cost before using it. In the next lesson, you'll learn several ways to get help when using WinCIM.

Lesson

Getting Help

In this lesson, you will learn how to get help using WinCIM.

Answering WinCIM Questions

When you have a question about using WinCIM, you can find the answer in a number of different ways:

- Use the built-in WinCIM Help menu.
- Click the Help button that's included in many dialog boxes.
- Pres the F1 key.
- Click the Help icon in the Ribbon.
- Post a question in the help forum.
- Call Customer Service.

Using WinCIM's Help System

You can get information about many subjects without connecting to CompuServe by using WinCIM's Help system. When you need help, press F1, or click the Help icon to get *context-sensitive help* (shown in Figure 6.1). A Help menu appears, giving information about whatever you are currently using in WinCIM.

Getting Help   31

Click this icon for help.

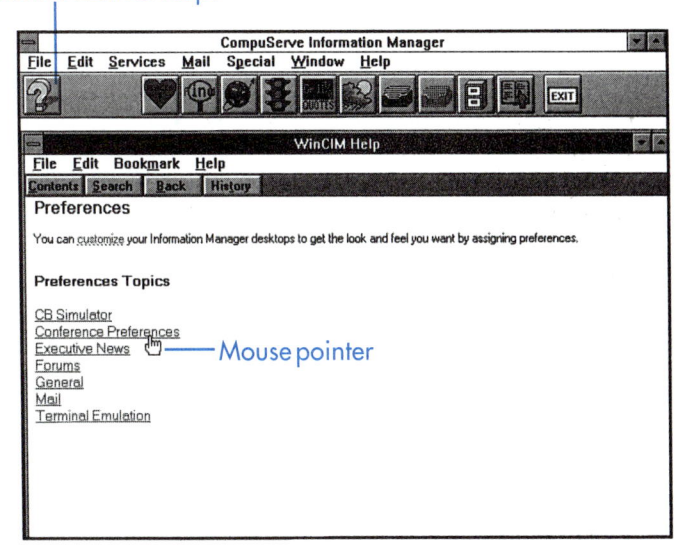

[Figure: CompuServe Information Manager window showing WinCIM Help with Preferences topics: CB Simulator, Conference Preferences, Executive News, Forums, General, Mail, Terminal Emulation. Mouse pointer indicated.]

Figure 6.1 The Help icon.

Context-Sensitive Help   Help for an operation you are performing or help for what's on-screen. For example, if you are using Favorite Places and become confused, click the Help icon. A help screen appears explaining its use.

Using the Help Menu

If context-sensitive help doesn't appear when you press F1 or click the Help icon, use the pull-down Help menu and search for information. Try using the Help table of contents now to find information about changing an entry in your address book:

1. Click Help on the menu bar.

2. Click Search for Help on. The Search dialog box appears (see Figure 6.2).

3. Type the word change in the text box at the cursor. All topics beginning with **change** appear in the list box below the text box.

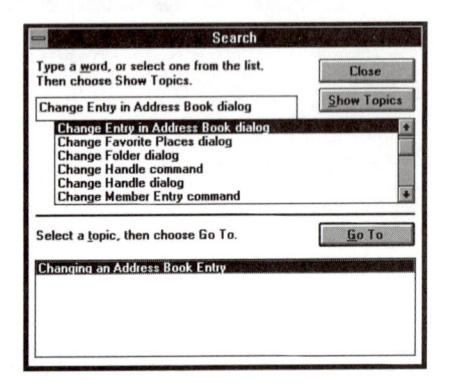

Figure 6.2 The Search dialog box.

4. Double-click Change Entry in Address Book dialog. WinCIM inserts this topic in the Go To box.

5. Click the Go To button to reach the Help screen you selected.

Notice that the cursor turns into a hand as it passes over certain areas of the Help screen (as shown in Figure 6.1). When the cursor looks like a hand, you can click the mouse button to bring up a Help balloon with an explanation about the feature the cursor is pointing to.

Getting Help 33

Getting Help Online

You may have a question that the built-in WinCIM Help system cannot answer. There are still many options left if you connect to CompuServe. Here you can:

- Search for information in one of the many forums (see Lesson 20).
- Post a question in one of the forums.
- Read frequently asked questions in Customer Service.
- Send a feedback message to Customer Service.
- Call a Customer Service Representative.

GO WCIMSUPPORT Use GO WCIMSUPPORT to get free help using WinCIM.

For example, suppose you are considering upgrading from an earlier version of WinCIM. Try searching for information about the upgrade in WinCIM Support, one of two free help forums. Follow these basic steps:

1. Click the Go icon. The Go dialog box appears.

2. Type WCIMSUPPORT in the Service text box.

3. Click OK. You connect to CompuServe and you enter the WinCIM Support Forum.

4. Click the Search Files icon (see Figure 6.3). The Search for Files dialog box opens.

5. Click in the Keywords text box.

6. Type the word upgrade and press Enter. The Library Search dialog box appears, listing files which provide information about upgrading.

Lesson 6

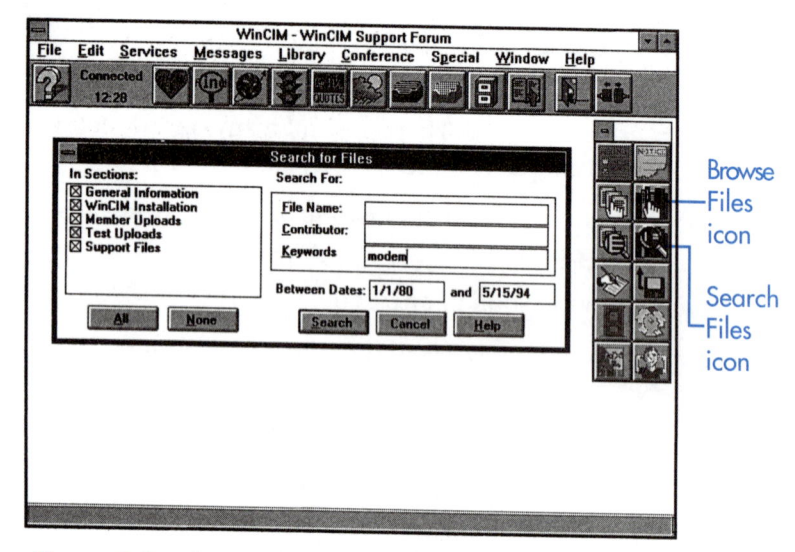

Figure 6.3 The WinCIM Support Forum.

Downloading Help Information

In the Library Search dialog box, take a moment to browse the subject headings and select one that interests you. Check the description of the file and download it for off-line reading:

1. Highlight a file that looks interesting.

2. Click the Description button to verify the contents.

3. Click the Mark button (if you don't want to download this file, click Close). The Save As dialog box appears, showing the file name and subdirectory where your file will be saved.

4. (Optional) Change the name of the file or the subdirectory to direct it to a different location.

5. Click OK. The Save As dialog box closes.

Getting Help 35

6. Click the Close button to return to the Library Search dialog box.

7. (Optional) Repeat Steps 2 through 6 to mark other files for downloading.

8. Click Library on the menu bar. The Library menu appears.

9. Click on the Retrieve Marked command. The Retrieve Marked Files box appears.

10. Click the Retrieve All button. A dialog box appears with a bar that shows you how much of each file is saved and how much has yet to be saved.

11. Click the Leave icon on the Ribbon.

12. Click the Disconnect icon to go offline. The file you retrieved is now in the DOWNLOAD subdirectory (unless you specified a different directory to save to). To open it and read it offline, see Lesson 7.

> **GO HELPFORUM** The CompuServe Help Forum is similar to the WinCIM Support Forum and covers issues about the online CompuServe Network Services.

Calling Customer Service

No matter how friendly these Help systems are, you may prefer to address your question to a human being. You can speak to a CompuServe Customer Service representative—if your call goes through. In the United States, the number is 1-800-848-8990. Be prepared to dial many times and wait on hold.

In this lesson, you learned several ways to get help on using WinCIM. In the next lesson, you will learn more about downloading files and reading them offline.

Lesson 7

Filing and Downloading Information

In this lesson, you will learn how to capture information using the File It button. You will also learn how to locate and open captured files.

Reversing the Flow

When connected to CompuServe, you see a lot of interesting information cross your screen. However, when you disconnect, it's all gone. If you want to save some information from the network, you can download the things you see and keep them stored in your own computer to view or use at a later time.

CompuServe provides several ways to download text and graphics files. In this lesson, we explore the easiest, most frequently available method: using the File It button (see Figure 7.1).

Filing and Downloading Information 37

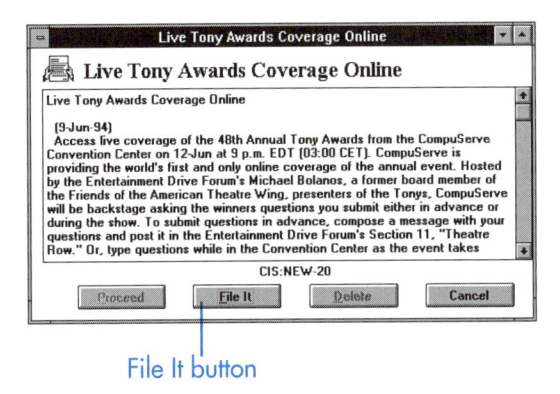

```
┌─────────────────────────────────────────┐
│  ▼  Live Tony Awards Coverage Online ▼▲ │
├─────────────────────────────────────────┤
│  🖨  Live Tony Awards Coverage Online   │
│ ┌─────────────────────────────────────┐ │
│ │ Live Tony Awards Coverage Online    │▲│
│ │                                     │ │
│ │ (9-Jun-94)                          │ │
│ │    Access live coverage of the 48th │ │
│ │ Annual Tony Awards from the CompuSe-│ │
│ │ rve Convention Center on 12-Jun at  │ │
│ │ 9 p.m. EDT (03:00 CET). CompuServe  │ │
│ │ is providing the world's first and  │ │
│ │ only online coverage of the annual  │ │
│ │ event. Hosted by the Entertainment  │ │
│ │ Drive Forum's Michael Bolanos, a    │ │
│ │ former board member of the Friends  │ │
│ │ of the American Theatre Wing,       │ │
│ │ presenters of the Tonys, CompuServe │ │
│ │ will be backstage asking the winners│ │
│ │ questions you submit either in      │ │
│ │ advance or during the show. To      │ │
│ │ submit questions in advance, compose│ │
│ │ a message with your questions and   │ │
│ │ post it in the Entertainment Drive  │ │
│ │ Forum's Section 11, "Theatre Row."  │ │
│ │ Or, type questions while in the     │ │
│ │ Convention Center as the event takes│▼│
│ └─────────────────────────────────────┘ │
│                       CIS:NEW-20        │
│  [ Proceed ]  [ File It ]  [ Delete ]  [ Cancel ] │
└─────────────────────────────────────────┘
                     │
                File It button
```

Figure 7.1   The File It button, which is found on many text screens.

Using the File It Button

The What's New This Week screen contains information about new services and features offered by CompuServe. Follow these steps to learn how to capture the What's New This Week list with the File It Button:

1. Click the Services menu.

2. Click What's New. You connect to CompuServe and the What's New This Week box appears.

3. Scan the items and double-click one to open it. The item appears in its own box with a File It button at the bottom.

4. Click the File It button. The Filing Cabinet dialog box appears, asking where you want this information stored.

5. Click Auto-Filed, if it isn't highlighted already.

6. Click the Save button. The Filing Cabinet dialog box disappears and a note appears at the bottom saying WinCIM saved the document.

7. Click the Disconnect icon on the Ribbon. You are now offline, but you can read the information you have downloaded.

Before you retrieve the file, you should know about the file structure used in WinCIM. Read the next section for information on the Filing Cabinet.

Using the Filing Cabinet

When you installed WinCIM, the program automatically created a number of subdirectories and sub-subdirectories. These are used as file folders in WinCIM to store your captured information.

> **Folders** Subdirectories inside the Filing Cabinet.

Plain English

Retrieving Files

Now, it's time to find the file that you stored in the Filing Cabinet. Make sure you are offline; then follow these steps:

1. Click Window on the menu bar.

2. Close the open windows by clicking Close All.

3. Click the Filing Cabinet icon on the Ribbon. The Filing Cabinet dialog box opens, showing the folders stored there.

Filing and Downloading Information

4. Double-click Auto-Filed then select the Auto-Field folder. The Auto-Filed folder opens and you can see the stored files (see Figure 7.2).

Auto-Filed folder

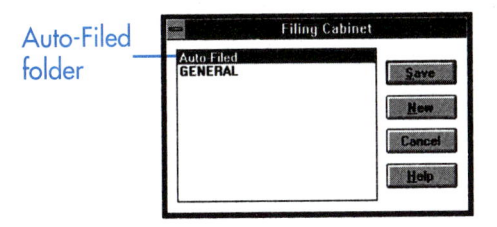

Figure 7.2 The Filing Cabinet dialog box.

5. Double-click the file you sent to the Auto-Filed folder from the What's New This Week dialog box. It opens and you can now read it offline.

6. Delete the file when you finish by clicking the Delete button at the bottom of the dialog box. A new dialog box appears asking you to verify the deletion.

7. Click Yes.

Filing information while online and reading it offline minimizes the expense of using CompuServe. However, it can be confusing finding files later. You may want to take some time to explore the directory structure of WinCIM so you can file and retrieve information easily.

In this lesson, you learned how to file information using the File It button and retrieve it from the Filing Cabinet. In the next lesson, you will learn to use Notepad to edit and print files.

Lesson 8

Editing and Printing a File with Notepad

This lesson will show you how to use the Windows Notepad accessory to open a file, edit the text, and print out the final document.

Using Notepad

WinCIM uses Windows' Notepad text editing program: a bare-bones program for creating and editing short files. If you want to go one step up from Notepad and do a little bit of *character formatting*, you can *export* the file to a more powerful word processing program, such as WordPerfect for Windows or Word for Windows.

> **Character Formatting** Character formatting is any change made to the characters'—or letters'—look. This would include the font (the size and shape of the letters) and whether the letters appear in bold or italic.
>
> *Plain English*

> **Exporting** Taking a file created in one program and sending it to another program.
>
> *Plain English*

Editing and Printing a File with Notepad   41

Learn Notepad for E-Mail, Too The editing commands used in Notepad are virtually the same as those used when writing e-mail (see Lesson 13). If you take the time to learn the shortcut keys, you can use them in both applications.

Getting to Know Notepad's Features

When you download information from CompuServe it's easy to read it in the In-Basket. But in some cases you want a printed copy. For printing files, and making minor changes to a document, use Notepad.

Notepad enables you to:

- Cut or copy text and paste it elsewhere in the same file or another file.
- Undo the last editing command.
- Automatically insert the time and date.
- Print out the contents of the file.

Remember Four Keys Notice that the shortcut keys for the four main commands—Undo (ALT+Z), Cut (ALT+X), Copy (ALT+C), and Paste (ALT+V)—are the four keys in the lower left of the keyboard. This might make it easier for you to remember them.

Opening a Document

To open a document in Notepad, first run WinCIM. Then follow these steps:

1. Click File on the menu bar.
2. Click Open. The Open dialog box appears.

Lesson 8

3. Double-click on CSERVE under the Directories section of the Open dialog box.

4. Double-click on the FCABINET subdirectory under the Directories section of the Open dialog box. A new list of subdirectories appears.

5. Double-click on the CABINET subdirectory under the Directories section of the Open dialog box. A new list of subdirectories appears.

6. Double-click on the FOLDER00.000 subdirectory under the Directories section of the Open dialog box.

7. Double-click in the File Name box, *.TXT is highlighted.

8. Type *.ART to see a list of files you've downloaded.

9. (Optional) To see a list of all the e-mail files you received, type *.PLX in the File Name box.

10. Press Enter. A list of files will appear.

11. Highlight one of the file names.

12. Press Enter. The file will open and appear in Notepad.

While the file in Notepad may look strangely formatted, this will be changed in the next section.

Using Word Wrap

Word wrap is a feature offered on most word processors. It means that the length of the lines automatically adjust to the right hand margin. The file now on your screen looks strange because word wrap is not automatically applied in Notepad. To select this feature, follow these steps:

Editing and Printing a File with Notepad 43

1. Click the Edit menu. The menu drops down, showing you the editing commands (see Figure 8.1).

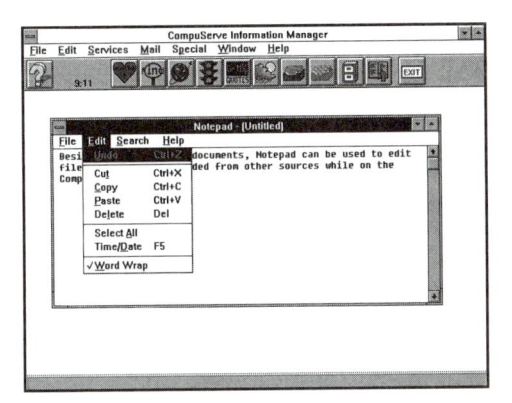

Figure 8.1 The Notepad window and Edit menu.

2. Click Word Wrap. The menu disappears and the text is formatted to fit inside the Notepad window.

There may be some other changes you want to make to the file before printing it. The basic editing commands in Notepad are covered in the next section.

Editing in Notepad

The Cut, Copy, and Paste commands may be familiar to you if you use a stand-alone word processor.

- **Cut** This feature removes text and stores it in the Clipboard.
- **Copy** This reproduces text in another area of the file.
- **Paste** This inserts text you have cut that is in the Clipboard.

> **Clipboard** The Clipboard is an area of windows where text is temporarily stored while you are editing a file. The text can then be retrieved—or copied—to another section of the document.

To cut or copy a phrase to the Clipboard and paste it somewhere else, follow these steps:

1. Select a word or phrase by dragging the mouse pointer over the text you want.

2. Click Edit on Notepad's menu bar.

3. Click Cut or Copy. Notepad cuts or copies the word or phrase to the Clipboard.

4. Move the cursor to the new location and click the left mouse button.

5. Click Edit on Notepad's menu bar.

6. Click Paste. Notepad pastes the text on the Clipboard into your document at the cursor position.

> **Fast Move**   To quickly move small amounts of text from a downloaded CompuServe file to your word processor, select the text and cut it to the Clipboard. Then switch to your word processor and select the Paste command. For information on switching to an open application, see the Windows Primer in the back of this book.

Undoing Mistakes

A useful feature of Notepad is the Undo command. Undo reverses the most recent editing command. Follow these steps to learn how Undo works:

1. Place your cursor somewhere in the text you've typed.

2. Press Ctrl+Backspace. Everything to the right of the cursor disappears. Don't panic; you can get the text back.

Editing and Printing a File with Notepad   45

3. Click Edit on the menu bar.

4. Click Undo. WinCIM replaces the text.

These steps are a good example of a mistake you may actually make in Notepad. If you use Word for Windows, you know the Ctrl+Backspace command deletes only one word. In Notepad, Ctrl+Backspace deletes everything to the right of the cursor. If you make a mistake like the one in this example, use Undo before you do anything else to correct the error.

Setting Up and Printing Files in Notepad

You may want to use Notepad to print files you download from CompuServe. Practice now by printing your text using these steps:

1. Click File on the menu bar.

2. If this is the first time you've used Notepad, click Print Setup. If it isn't, skip to step 5.

3. In the Print Setup dialog box, click Portrait if it isn't already selected (as shown in Figure 8.2). This will print the file vertically on the page in the normal manner of most letters and written documents.

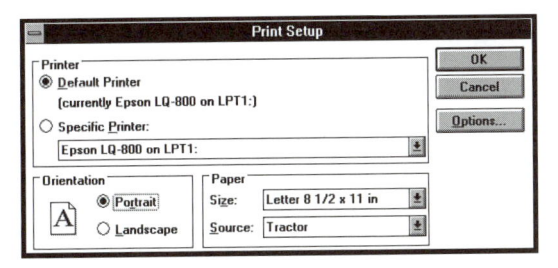

Figure 8.2 The Print Setup dialog box in Notepad.

Lesson 8

4. Close the Print Setup dialog box by clicking OK.

5. Click File on the menu bar.

6. Click Print. Notepad prints the file.

In this lesson, you learned how to create, edit, and print a file using Notepad. In the next lesson, you will learn how to view news and weather reports.

Lesson 9

Viewing News and Weather Reports

In this lesson, you will learn how to view news and weather reports from CompuServe's Basic Services window.

Keeping Up-to-Date with CompuServe

Viewing news and weather reports on CompuServe offers several advantages over reading them in a newspaper. For instance, you can:

- Read only the most up-to-date news reports.
- Scan for specific topics.
- View color weather maps of many areas around the world.
- Retrieve, store, and print out articles.

Viewing News Reports

The most comprehensive news sources in CompuServe are in extended services and are expensive to use. However, if all you want is a quick look at the main stories, go to the Associated Press Online news summaries. They are timely and informative, and carry no extra charge.

To read the top stories of the hour, make sure the Services window is showing on-screen. Then:

Lesson 9

1. Click the News icon in the Services group window (shown in Figure 9.1). The News/Weather/Sports window opens, displaying the available services.

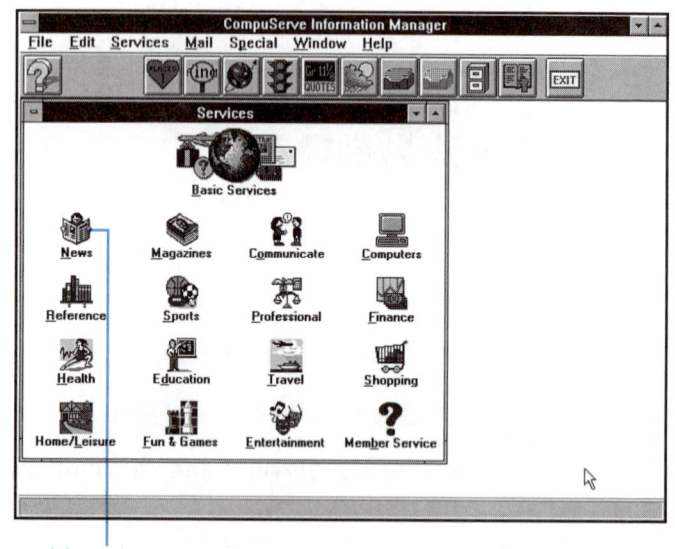

News icon

Figure 9.1 The News icon found in the Services group window.

2. Double-click Associated Press Online. WinCIM connects you to CompuServe, and the Alert dialog box containing copyright information appears.

3. Click Proceed. The AP Online window opens containing news selections.

4. (Optional) The first time you select Associated Press Online, two more dialog boxes appear asking you to agree to certain copyright terms. Basically, you must agree not to reprint and sell articles contained here. To proceed:

Viewing News and Weather Reports 49

- In the first box press Y if you agree, and select OK.

- In the Alert dialog box for AP Online, select Proceed.

5. Double-click Latest News-Updated Hourly. A menu appears that lists reports with their release times. CompuServe highlights the latest news, but you can highlight another.

6. Double-click the highlighted choice. A window appears, titled "AP Top News At —," showing the release time (see Figure 9.2).

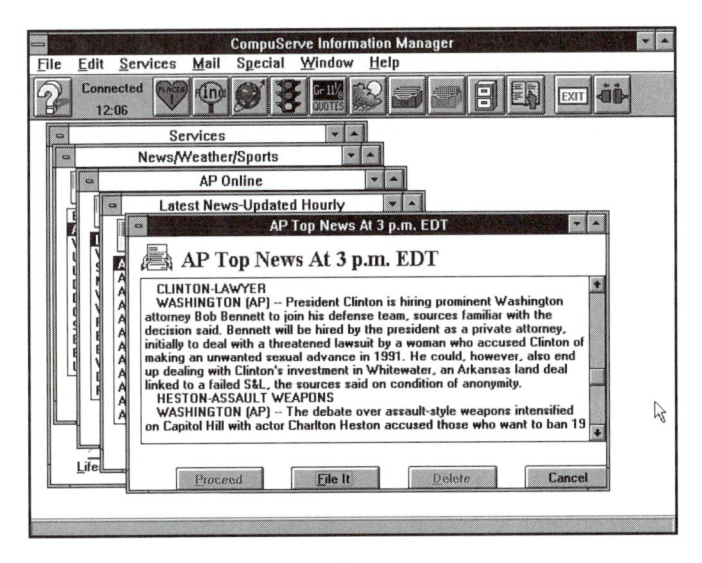

Figure 9.2 An Associated Press top news story.

7. Read the item online (or see Lesson 7 to learn how to capture information and read it offline).

8. Click the Cancel button for each open box; there should be three.

Lesson 9

Closing Screens Sometimes, your screen becomes littered with open windows, which you must close to return to the main menu. To close them one at a time, double-click on the Control-menu boxes. Close all of the windows in one step by opening the Window menu and choosing Close All.

Viewing Weather Reports

CompuServe provides weather reports for many locations and conditions. Follow these steps for up-to-date information any time:

1. Click the Basic Services icon from the Services window. Then, select the News/Weather/Sports option in the CompuServe dialog box. The News/Weather/Sports window opens.

2. Double-click Weather. The CompuServe Weather Reports dialog box opens, identifying your location (see Figure 9.3).

Click here to enter a new location.

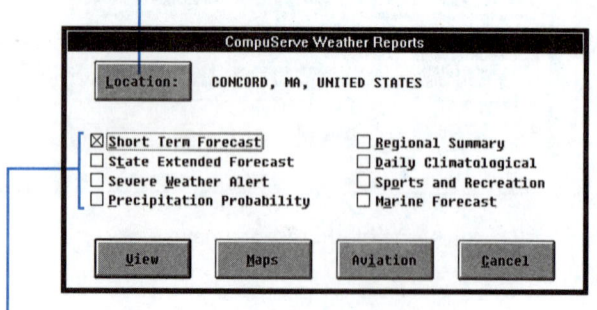

```
┌─────────── CompuServe Weather Reports ───────────┐
│  ┌─────────┐                                     │
│  │Location:│  CONCORD, MA, UNITED STATES         │
│  └─────────┘                                     │
│                                                  │
│   ⊠ Short Term Forecast      ☐ Regional Summary  │
│   ☐ State Extended Forecast  ☐ Daily Climatological │
│   ☐ Severe Weather Alert     ☐ Sports and Recreation │
│   ☐ Precipitation Probability ☐ Marine Forecast  │
│                                                  │
│    ┌────┐   ┌────┐   ┌────────┐   ┌──────┐      │
│    │View│   │Maps│   │Aviation│   │Cancel│      │
│    └────┘   └────┘   └────────┘   └──────┘      │
└──────────────────────────────────────────────────┘
```

Select the type of report you want.

Figure 9.3   The CompuServe Weather Reports dialog box.

Viewing News and Weather Reports   51

3. (Optional) You can click the Location button and type in a different city, state, and/or country for weather information about that area. (CompuServe provides weather reports on many cities worldwide.)

4. (Optional) Click OK if you entered a new location. If not, skip to Step 5.

5. Choose the type of report(s) you want to look at by clicking on the report descriptions. Short Term Forecast is the default, and you can add others. Each report that has an X in its box will be shown.

6. Click the View button. CompuServe displays a report.

7. (Optional) If you selected more than one report, click the Next button to view the next report.

8. Return to the News/Weather/Sports window by clicking Cancel in the two weather dialog boxes.

Looking at Weather Maps

CompuServe also provides colorful weather maps showing temperatures, precipitation rates, and weather forecasts. To view the maps:

1. Go to the News/Weather/Sports window, if you aren't already there.

2. Double-click Weather.

3. Click the Maps button. Depending on the baud rate of your modem, the maps may take up to 30 seconds to appear. A map is shown in Figure 9.4.

52   Lesson 9

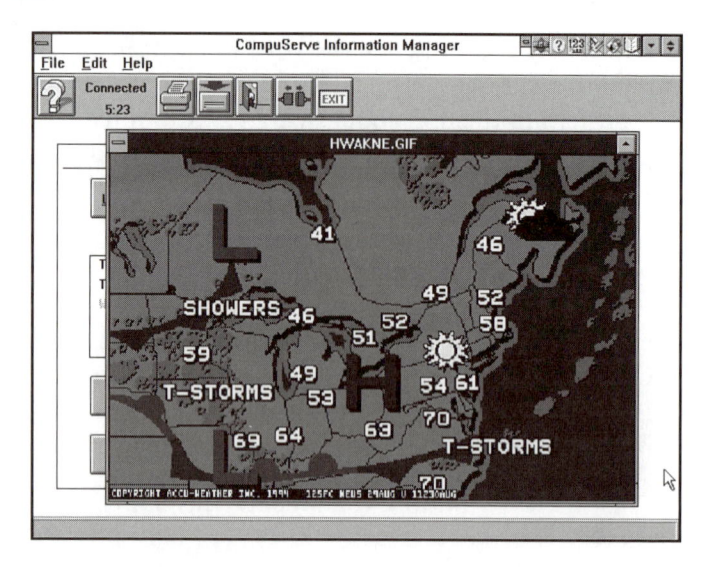

Figure 9.4   A CompuServe weather map, copyright Accu-Weather, Inc.

4. When you finish with the map, double-click the window's Control-menu box in the upper left corner.

   Exiting Weather Maps   When you exit a weather map, CompuServe asks if you want to save the map. There is usually no reason to do this; so click No to return to the main menu.

   Cut to the Weather   To skip the news and go right to the weather, click the Weather icon on the Ribbon. The Weather dialog box appears (see Figure 9.5). Use it to view weather reports or maps for any location.

Viewing News and Weather Reports 53

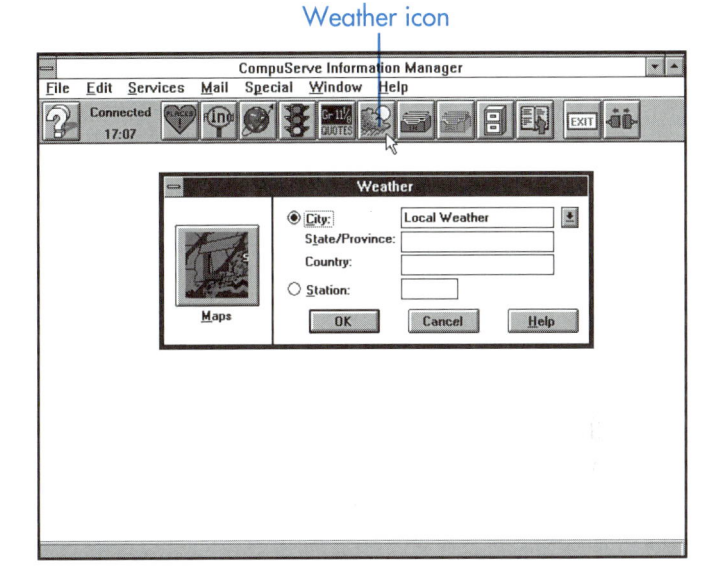

Figure 9.5 The Weather icon and Weather dialog box.

In this lesson, you learned how to view news and weather reports. In the next lesson, you will learn how to use CompuServe's online encyclopedia and powerful phone directory.

Lesson 10

Using the Electronic Library

In this lesson, you will learn how to use the online encyclopedia and a national phone directory.

Using CompuServe's Reference Sources

The Academic Encyclopedia is the reference staple of many households. CompuServe offers an electronic version of this long-time favorite. In many ways, the online encyclopedia is easier and faster to use than the bound version.

CompuServe offers other reference sources. In basic services, members can:

- Access articles from Consumer Reports.
- Obtain information about colleges across the country.
- Retrieve basic health-related information.
- Quickly look up words in the American Heritage Dictionary.

In extended services, much more information is available. You can:

- Obtain demographic figures and government reports.
- Retrieve the latest articles about computer-related subjects.

Using the Electronic Library

- Search *databases* for magazine articles.
- Obtain consumer information to aid in car buying.

> **Database** Information stored in a specially designed computer file. Databases make it possible to easily retrieve information and manipulate it in many ways. *Plain English*

You could find much of the above listed information in a public library, although it would be hard to locate and time-consuming to retrieve. Using the online database found on CompuServe is fast and convenient.

Another important advantage of doing online research is that the information is up-to-date. For example, CompuServe and Grolier revise the Academic American Encyclopedia four times a year.

Using the Electronic Encyclopedia

To practice online research methods, let's search for information about personal computers in the encyclopedia. From WinCIM's startup screen, follow these steps:

1. Click the Browse icon on the Ribbon. The main Service window appears.

2. Click the Reference icon. You connect to CompuServe, and the Reference menu lists all reference sources.

3. Double-click Academic American Encyclopedia, and a Groliers menu for the encyclopedia appears.

4. Double-click Search Encyclopedia. An untitled box appears asking for the search term.

5. Type computer in the Search term box and press Enter. ("Personal computers" would be too specific at this point.) A list of computer-related articles appears.

Lesson 10

6. Scroll down to **computer, personal** and double-click on it. A new screen (shown in Figure 10.1) gives the main headings of this subject.

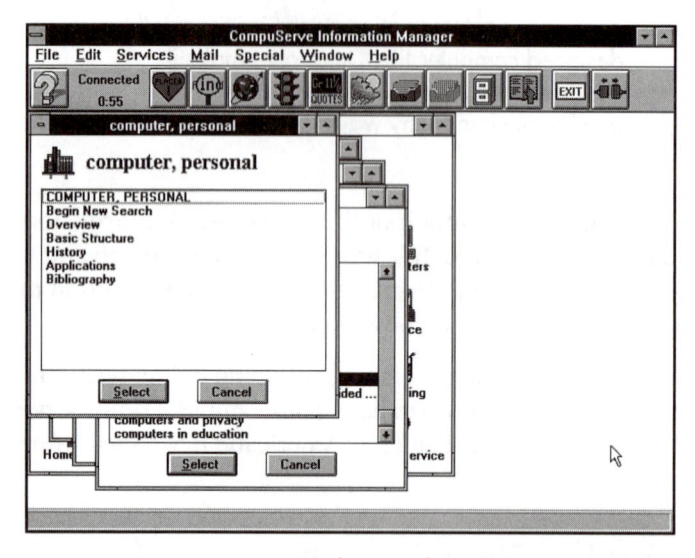

Figure 10.1 Screens used to reach an article on computers.

7. Double-click Overview. A general description of the personal computer appears (see Figure 10.2). It's a good idea to use the Overview button to verify that you are in the right general area before continuing with further research.

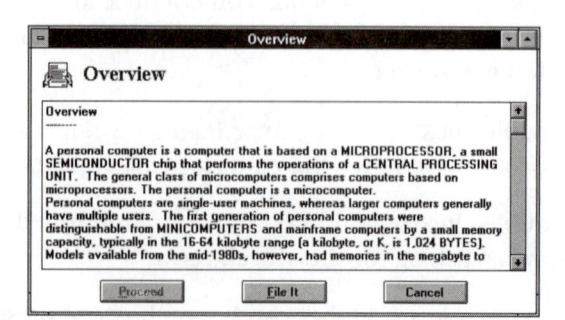

Figure 10.2 A general description appears in the Overview window.

Using the Electronic Library

8. Click Cancel in the four dialog boxes to return to the main reference menu.

> **Smart Search** Make sure to use the singular form of the topic you're searching for. If you're unsure of the spelling, type in just the first five letters, and a list of subjects that match the first five letters appears.

Searching for Missing Persons

How would you like to find the address and phone number of a long lost friend? A distant relative? A former business contact? Phone*File, in extended services, enables you to do this. It contains entries for 80 million U.S. households and lets you search these entries in a number of ways.

Before we try a sample search, think of the name of someone you want to find. It's best if the person has an unusual last name.

It's easy to carry out a sample Phone*File search. Following these steps will cost you about 75 cents:

1. Double-click Name/Address/Phone Directories under the Extended Reference Products heading in the Reference menu box. A new Name/Address/Phone Directories menu offers several directories to choose from.

2. Double-click Phone*File.

3. A CompuServe menu box appears listing several choices relating to Phone*File. Select Access Phone*File($).

Lesson 10

4. An Alert box appears, notifying you of additional costs.

5. Click the Proceed button. You enter *terminal emulation* mode as you connect to Phone*File (shown in Figure 10.3). CompuServe now offers you several ways to search.

> **Terminal Emulation Mode** When your computer acts like the terminal for another computer system. This happens when you are in a service that does not support WinCIM's graphical environment.
>
> *Plain English*

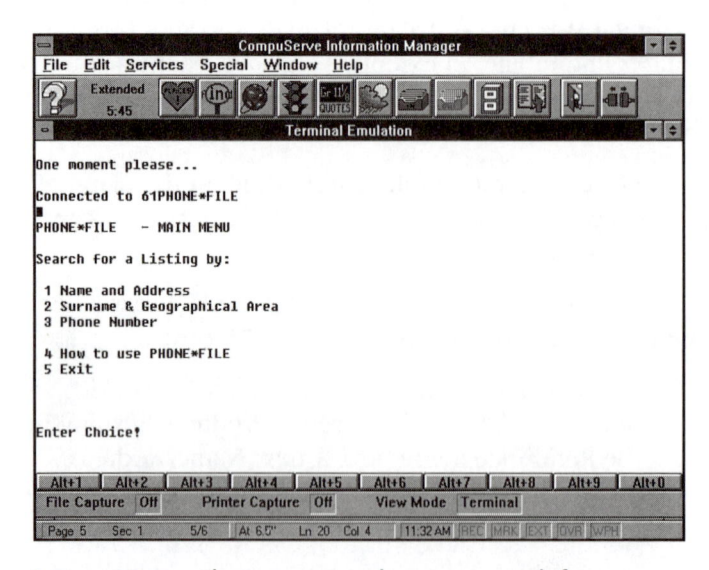

```
                    CompuServe Information Manager
 File  Edit  Services  Special  Window  Help

                          Terminal Emulation

One moment please...

Connected to 61PHONE*FILE

PHONE*FILE    - MAIN MENU

Search for a Listing by:

  1 Name and Address
  2 Surname & Geographical Area
  3 Phone Number

  4 How to use PHONE*FILE
  5 Exit


Enter Choice!

 Alt+1   Alt+2   Alt+3   Alt+4   Alt+5   Alt+6   Alt+7   Alt+8   Alt+9   Alt+0
 File Capture  Off    Printer Capture  Off    View Mode  Terminal
 Page 5  Sec 1    5/6   At 6.0"  Ln 20  Col 4   11:32 AM
```

Figure 10.3 There are several ways to search for a person using Phone*File.

Using the Electronic Library

6. Press the number 2 and press Enter to choose Surname & Geographical Area.

7. Press 2 and press Enter to choose State Only. (If you know the city of the person you are searching for, choose the city instead.)

8. Enter the two character state abbreviation, and press Enter.

9. Type only the person's last name, and press Enter. You can now verify and change the information if it's incorrect.

10. Press Enter to begin the search. CompuServe displays the number of listings found.

11. Press Enter to read the listings one screen at a time.

12. Click the Leave icon on the Ribbon to quickly exit Phone*File. Before disconnecting, a dialog box appears showing how much the search cost.

> **Time Is Money!** Say you find 45 listings for the name you entered. You begin scrolling through them and suddenly find you can't stop! In that situation, type **top** or **menu** at the next prompt, and you will return to the opening menu.

Phone*File is just one example of the information you can find through CompuServe's extended services. Take the time to read the descriptions of these services, usually labeled as **Introduction** or **Description**. The introductions are often free and describe the services offered before you pay for them.

In this lesson, you learned how to search for information in the online encyclopedia and how to locate a friend in Phone*File. In the next lesson, you will discover more about the powerful databases found in CompuServe.

Lesson 11

Searching a Magazine Database

In this lesson, you will learn how to find information in a magazine database.

Doing Research on CompuServe

When you connect to CompuServe, it's like having a subscription to thousands of magazines and newspapers. Luckily, you don't receive them all in the mail. However, you do have access to them electronically—in many ways, this is even better. Instead of thumbing through all those pages, you can quickly search for exactly the information you want.

What's Available?

CompuServe provides access to thousands of newspapers and magazines through a variety of databases (for a definition of database, see Lesson 10). These are either trade magazines (covering a specific industry), general interest magazines, or newspapers with articles on all subjects.

When choosing a database to search, base your decision on these elements:

- **Cost**   Most databases on CompuServe are in extended services. Searching for information can be expensive. However, some databases are cheaper than others. Always check the pricing information first.

- **Entries** If your search request is very obscure, you will want the broadest possible range of entries. Choose a database that accesses the most magazines, newspapers, journals, and reports.

- **Method of Use** You cannot search all the databases the same way. You have to access some of them while in terminal emulation mode (see Lesson 10), but in some you can use the regular CIM format. (Databases in the CIM format have (CIM) after their title in the menu boxes.) Pick a database that is easy to use, and you'll spend less time trying to find what you need.

> **Browse for Free** Although most databases are in extended services, you can learn what they have to offer for free. Before being charged to enter the database, you will often find an information screen. This tells you what sources you can search and all the costs.

Using Magazine Database Plus (CIM)

One of the friendliest databases on CompuServe is Magazine Database Plus (CIM). This service accesses some 140 magazines, journals, and reports and has over 280,000 articles. Magazine Database Plus (CIM) updates the publications weekly; it's a great resource.

We'll run through an example to familiarize you with the process. Before we go online and do a sample search, think of a subject that interests you, but have had trouble finding information about. Substitute your topic for the one used here. (In the following example, searching for information will not cost extra. However, if you view or retrieve an article, it will cost you $1.50.)

Searching a Magazine Database 63

GO MAGDB To quickly go to Magazine Database Plus (CIM), use GO MAGDB.

To search for information in Magazine Database Plus (CIM) follow these steps:

1. Make sure the Services window is open by clicking the Browse icon on the Ribbon. The Services window opens.

2. Click the Reference icon in the Services window. You connect to CompuServe, and the Reference menu box opens listing all the reference services available.

3. Scroll down to **Magazine Database Plus**.

4. Double-click Magazine Database Plus. The Magazine Database Plus menu box opens.

5. Double-click Access Magazine Database Plus (CIM)($). An Alert screen appears with introductory information.

6. Click Proceed. Another introductory screen appears.

7. Click OK. The Welcome to Magazine Database Plus dialog box appears. Notice that Magazine Database Plus (CIM) highlights QuickSearch (see Figure 11.1).

```
Welcome To Magazine Database Plus

        Select An Action
QuickSearch
Reference Number Retrieval
PowerSearch
Usage Report


      OK         Cancel
```

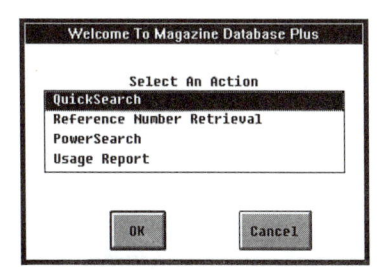

Figure 11.1 Magazine Database Plus (CIM) highlights QuickSearch automatically in the Welcome dialog box.

Beginning a Search

You can type in a word or phrase that describes the subject you're seeking information about. If you have trouble locating information on a subject, try an alternate key word or one that is more general.

1. Double-click QuickSearch. The QuickSearch dialog box opens (see Figure 11.2).

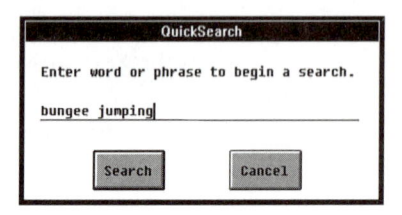

Figure 11.2 Type the subject you are seeking in the QuickSearch box.

2. Type in a word or phrase that describes the subject you're searching for information on.

3. Click Search. One of two things will happen:

- If the database has articles on this subject, the Subject Guide dialog box appears (see Figure 11.3).

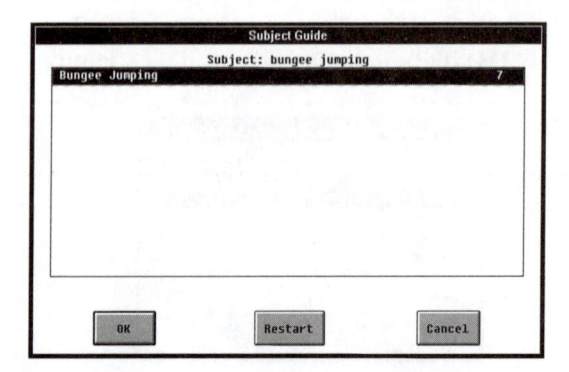

Figure 11.3 The Subject Guide Box shows the number of articles found.

Searching a Magazine Database 65

- If there are no articles, a Related Subject Entries Found dialog box appears (see Figure 11.4). From here, you can click Cancel to start the search again, or click OK to see an alternate subject list.

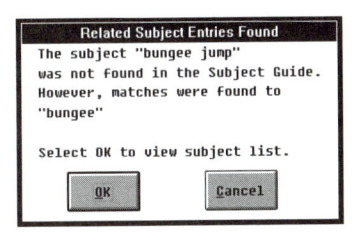

Figure 11.4 Items that partially match the desired keyword.

4. If you're in the Subject Guide dialog box, click OK. A summarized listing of articles appears in the Citations dialog box (see Figure 11.5).

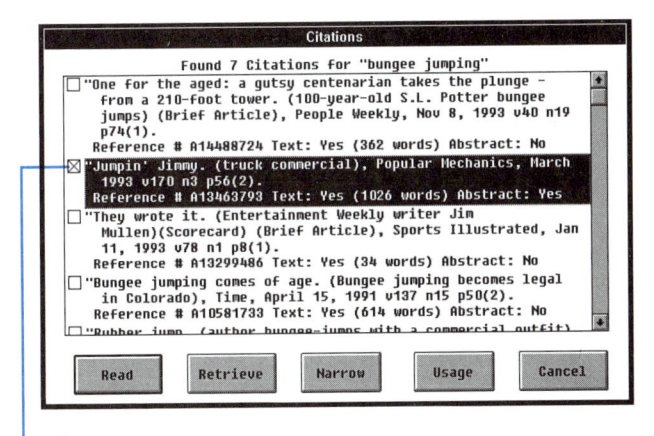

Selection box

Figure 11.5 Magazine Database Plus (CIM) summarizes articles in the Citations dialog box.

Viewing and Retrieving Articles

In the Citations dialog box, there are several option buttons across the bottom:

- **Read**   Displays the article (at a $1.50 charge).

- **Retrieve**   Downloads the article and you can read it off-line (for $1.50).

- **Narrow**   You can choose another key word to narrow your search.

- **Usage**   Provides a running total of your current costs.

To read or download an article, follow these steps (this will cost you $1.50):

1. Move the mouse pointer to the box at the left of the article description and click. An X appears in the Selection box (see Figure 11.5).

2. Click the Read button. The article appears in a Selected Documents dialog box (see Figure 11.6). If the article looks interesting and you want to keep a copy of it, proceed to step 3 to download it. Or skip to Step 6 to disconnect.

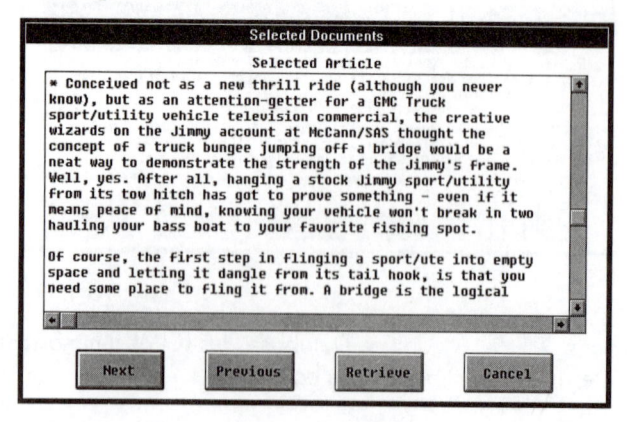

Figure 11.6   The full text of the article.

Searching a Magazine Database

Inside Moves If you've selected several articles to read, you can move between them without going back to the Citations dialog box. Just use the Next and Previous buttons along the bottom of the Selected Documents dialog box.

3. Click the Retrieve button. A Save As screen appears.

4. Click OK and the Articles to Retrieve box appears.

5. Click OK to download the article.

6. Click the Disconnect icon on the Ribbon to leave the database and CompuServe.

Disappearing Text To read articles in Magazine Database Plus (CIM), you have to select them by putting an X in the Selection box. Highlighting does not select an entry; the X in the box is the only way to select an entry.

While Magazine Database Plus (CIM) is fast and convenient, it is expensive. Furthermore, Magazine Database Plus (CIM) only charges if you read or download articles.

In this lesson, you learned how to search for and retrieve articles from a magazine database. In the next lesson, CompuServe's e-mail system will be introduced.

Lesson 12

Setting Up Your Address Book

In this lesson, you will learn how to look up the address of another CompuServe member and add it to your Address Book.

What Is the Address Book?

Your electronic Address Book is just like a paper address book. It holds the CompuServe *addresses* of people you contact frequently. You can use the Address Book to quickly find the address for the person to whom you are sending an electronic mail (e-mail) message. When you receive e-mail, you can copy the sender's name and address into your Address Book. (See Lessons 13 and 14 for more information on sending and receiving e-mail.)

Online Addresses The CompuServe *address* is the same as the user ID number: five digits, a comma, and more digits. For mail to reach another CompuServe member, this address is all you need. Someone can send mail to you via the Internet by adding @COMPUSERVE.COM after your user ID number. For example, if you use America OnLine and you want to send e-mail to someone at Alpha Books, you would use this CompuServe address: 73353,2061@COMPUSERVE.COM.

Setting Up Your Address Book 69

When you create an e-mail message, you must include an address so the message gets to the right person. If your Address Book contains the address of the person you are sending the message to, all you have to do is click on the address. You don't have to type in the address of the person each time you send him mail.

Adding an Address to the Address Book

If you know a person's address and you want to add it to your Address Book, follow these steps:

1. Click the Address Book icon in the Ribbon. The Address Book dialog box appears.

2. Click the Add button. The Add to Address Book dialog box appears, as shown in Figure 12.1.

Enter additional information here.   Address Book icon

Address Book dialog box

Enter the person's name and address in the text boxes.

Click the Add button to add a new address.

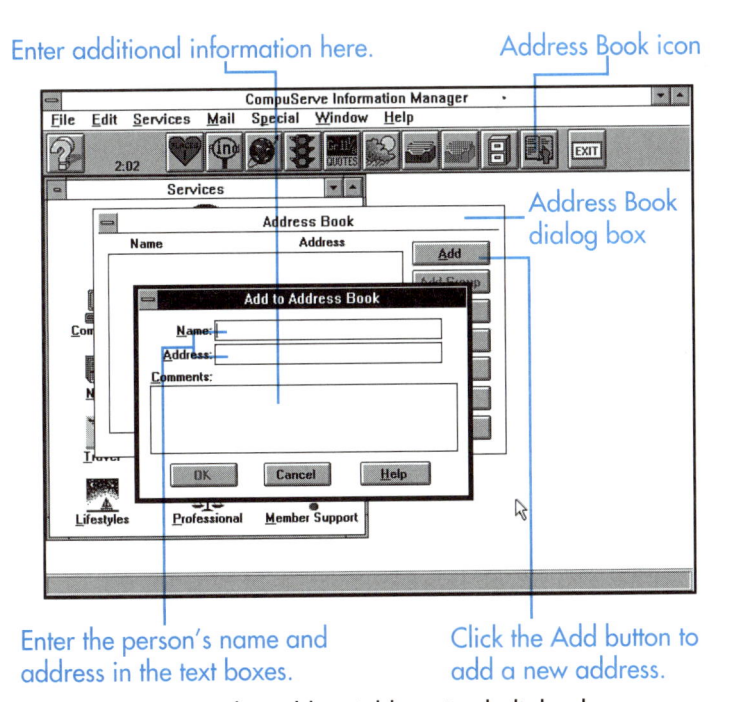

Figure 12.1 The Add to Address Book dialog box.

3. Type the person's name and address in the appropriate text boxes.

4. (Optional) Add any important information in the Comments box.

5. Click OK. The person's address appears in your Address Book.

6. Click OK to close the Address Book.

Looking Up a Member's Address

If you don't know the address of the person you want to send an e-mail message to, it's easy to look it up in CompuServe's Member Directory. To find the address of another CompuServe member, follow these instructions:

1. Click Mail on the menu bar.

2. Click Member Directory on the pull-down menu. The Search Member Directory dialog box appears.

3. Fill in as many blanks as you can. The more information you provide, the better the chance of finding the person you are looking for.

4. Click Search. If you are not already online, WinCIM connects you and searches the membership directory.

If you provided correct information for a registered member, a new dialog box appears with the names and CompuServe address of all members matching the data you entered in step 3 (see Figure 12.2).

Setting Up Your Address Book 71

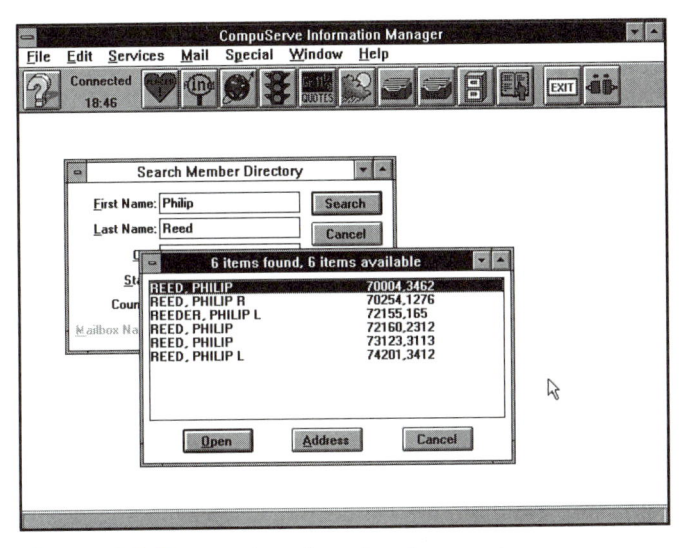

Figure 12.2 Members found in the search.

If CompuServe finds more matching entries than it is able to show you, a dialog box appears asking you to narrow the search. Click OK to close the dialog box; then enter more information about the person you are looking for, and click Search again.

Copying Member Addresses to the Address Book

If you did not include a city and state in your search, the names of several members may appear in the dialog box. To find more information about the person you want to contact and copy their name to your Address Book, follow these steps:

1. Double-click the name you think is correct. A Member Information dialog box appears, displaying that person's city, state, country, and CompuServe ID number.

2. Do one of the following:

- If this isn't the right person, click the Cancel button then repeat step 1.

- If this is the person you're looking for, click the Address button to enter the information in your Address Book. The Add Member to Address Book dialog box appears.

3. (Optional) Enter any additional information about the person in the Comments box.

4. Click OK. WinCIM enters the information in your Address Book.

5. Click Cancel in the next three dialog boxes to return to the Services dialog box.

Shortcut to Addresses You can quickly bring up the Address Book by pressing CTRL+A.

Managing the Address Book

After you copy a member's address to your Address Book, you'll probably want to check to make sure it's actually there. To verify that WinCim entered the name and address, follow these steps:

1. Click the Address Book icon. The Address Book dialog box appears.

2. Scroll down to the alphabetical listing of the name you copied.

3. If you do not find the name, return to Step 1 of the previous section and begin the process again.

Setting Up Your Address Book

There are several options available to you from the Address Book dialog box (shown in Figure 12.3). You can add more addresses or edit the Address Book by clicking these buttons:

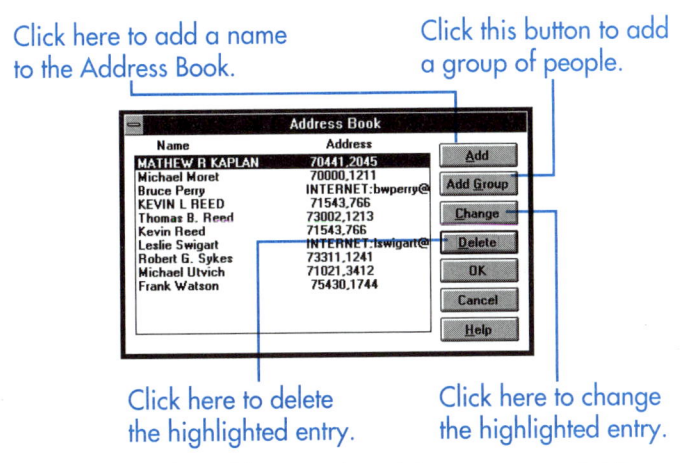

Click here to add a name to the Address Book.

Click this button to add a group of people.

Name	Address
MATHEW R KAPLAN	70441,2045
Michael Moret	70000,1211
Bruce Perry	INTERNET:bwperry@
KEVIN L REED	71543,766
Thomas B. Reed	73002,1213
Kevin Reed	71543,766
Leslie Swigart	INTERNET:lswigart@
Robert G. Sykes	73311,1241
Michael Utvich	71021,3412
Frank Watson	75430,1744

Buttons: Add, Add Group, Change, Delete, OK, Cancel, Help

Click here to delete the highlighted entry.

Click here to change the highlighted entry.

Figure 12.3 The Address Book and the options available.

- **Add** Adds a name and address to your Address Book.

- **Add Group** Defines a group of people to whom you frequently send copies of the same message (see Lesson 13 for more information).

- **Change** Updates the Address Book if information about a member changes.

- **Delete** Removes a name from the Address Book.

If you do not plan to look up any more addresses, you should disconnect from the network. (Click the Disconnect icon on the Ribbon.) You can open and modify the Address Book offline, so there's no reason to keep paying online charges.

Lesson 12

In this lesson, you learned how to look up CompuServe addresses of other members and add them to your Address Book. In the next lesson, you will learn how to create an e-mail message and send it to a person in your Address Book using the CompuServe Mail system.

Lesson 13

Sending E-Mail

In this lesson, you'll learn how to create and send electronic mail to other CompuServe members.

What Is E-mail?

E-mail, or *electronic mail*, is any written message sent between two computer terminals. You can send these messages via a modem to arrive almost instantly. The CompuServe e-mail system enables you to send messages to other CompuServe members, to people with an Internet address.

CompuServe Mail Features

The CompuServe mail system is quite versatile, and enables you to do many things, including:

- Create multiple messages and send them all at once.
- Send a single message to multiple recipients.
- Transfer a computer file to another CompuServe member.
- Receive, sort, and store messages.

The mail system also enables you to create a *forum* message that CompuServe members who share an interest in a topic can read. You can read about forums and forum messages in Lessons 20 and 21.

Locating the Mail Icons

CompuServe's main Ribbon contains four icons that are shortcuts to using the mail system: In-Basket, Out-Basket, Filing Cabinet, and Address Book (see Figure 13.1). When you go online and a message is waiting for you, the Mail icon, which looks like a mailbox, appears on the ribbon. (See the next lesson for information about other mail icons.)

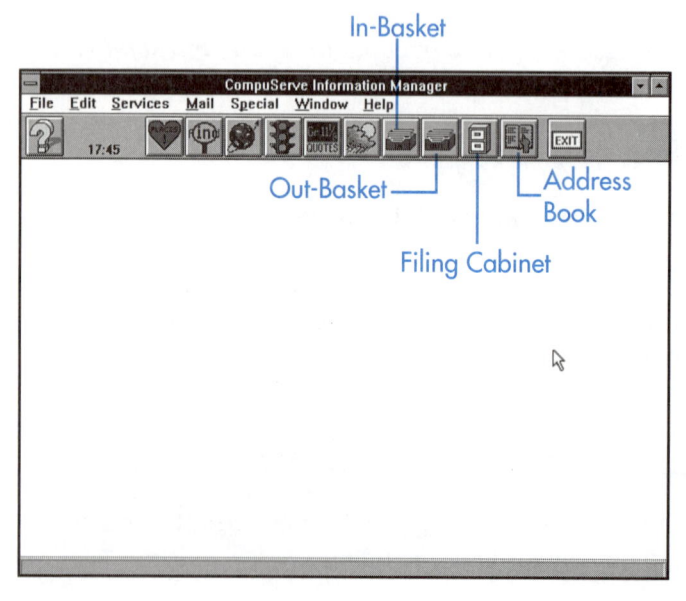

Figure 13.1 Use these icons to navigate the mail system.

Creating the Message

There are basically four steps in creating a mail message. First, you choose the recipient. Then, you give the message a subject. Third, you enter the text for the message. Finally, you select options for the message.

If you're paying for connect time, it's a good idea to create a message while you're off-line and temporarily store it in the *Out-Basket* until you're ready to send it.

Sending E-Mail

The Out-Basket For temporary storage of messages or files that you can send sometime in the future. Storing files in the Out-Basket enables you to create a number of messages and send them all at once.

Step 1: Selecting the Recipient

Before you create a message, you must first select the person you want to send it to. You can select someone from your Address Book, or you can type in the person's name and address.

To select the recipient from your Address Book, follow these instructions:

1. Click Mail on the menu bar. The Mail menu opens.

2. Click Create Mail. The Recipient List dialog box opens, which includes the Address Book list box (see Figure 13.2).

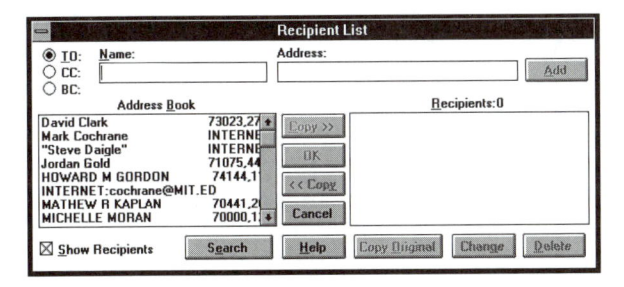

Figure 13.2 Use this dialog box to select recipients to receive mail.

3. Double-click on the name. (You may have to use the scroll bars to see it.) It's added to the Recipients list box on the right.

4. Click OK. The Recipient List box disappears, revealing the Create Mail dialog box (see Figure 13.3).

Lesson 13

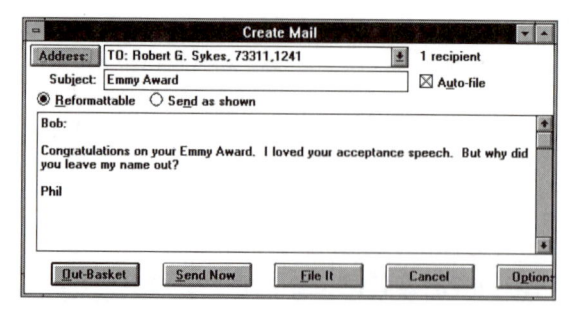

Figure 13.3 Create e-mail messages in this box.

One Message, Many Recipients WinCIM makes it easy to send copies of e-mail to many recipients. In the Recipient List box, double-click the name of every person you want to include. The names will all appear in the box on the right. WinCIM can send the message simultaneously to everyone on the list.

If the person you want to send mail to is not in your Address Book, follow these steps:

1. Click Mail on the menu bar. The Mail menu opens.

2. Click Create Mail. The Recipient List dialog box opens (shown in Figure 13.2).

3. In the Name text box, enter the person's name.

4. In the Address text box, enter the person's CompuServe address.

5. Click the Add button. WinCIM adds the person to the Recipients list box.

6. (Optional) If you want to add the person to your Address Book, click the <<Copy button. WinCIM copies the person's name and address to the Address Book list box.

7. Click OK. The Recipient List dialog box disappears, and the Create Mail dialog box is on-screen.

If you have been following either set of steps in this section, your cursor should now be in the Subject box, which brings us to the next step in creating a mail message.

Step 2: Entering a Subject

The last section's instructions brought you to the Subject text box of the Create Mail dialog box. In this text box, you need to enter a subject for the message. This is the "title" of the mail message; it will appear at the top of the mail window when the recipient views the message.

You can give your message any subject name—as long as it is eighty characters or less. When you finish entering a subject, press Tab and the cursor will move into the main box. (You can also just click in the main box to move the cursor.)

> **Subject Required** WinCIM requires you to provide a subject for each e-mail message. If you don't, you won't be able to click the Send Now button to send the mail.

Step 3: Entering Text

As you create an e-mail message, you have only basic editing commands to work with. Once you have typed in some text, you can move or copy words and sentences to other sections of the message. You can use commands found on the Edit pull-down menu to edit your text.

Editing in the Create Mailbox is nearly the same as editing in Notepad. See Lesson 8 for a complete description of how to edit and print text using Notepad.

Step 4: Considering Your Options

Before you send your message, you can apply several options to it by clicking the Options button in the bottom right corner of the Create Mail dialog box. This opens the Message Options dialog box, which offers these features (see Figure 13.4):

- **Importance**   Use this option to indicate the level of urgency of the message.

- **Release Date**   Specify when you want the message sent.

- **Expiration Date**   Specify when you want the message removed from the network, if it is still unread by the recipient on that date.

- **Receipt**   Click this check box if you want ComputServe to notify you when the recipient gets the message.

- **Sensitivity**   Specify that the content of the message is either normal, personal, private, or confidential.

- **Payment Method**   Designate that you will pay the mailing charges, the recipient will pay the mailing charges, or the charges will be split between you both (This option is only available if you're on the Standard Pricing Plan.)

Indicate the importance of the message here.

Determine the nature of the message here.

Enter the date you want to send the message here.

Enter the date you want the unread message to be deleted from the network.

Select a payment method.

Check this box for notification when the recipient gets the message.

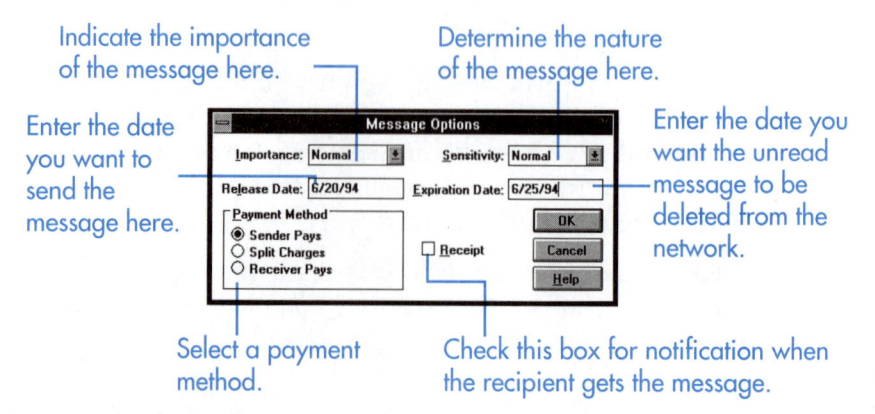

Figure 13.4   The Message Options dialog box for e-mail.

Sending the Message

When you have finished creating the message and you've selected the options you want, it's time to send it. You can send the message in two ways:

- The easiest way is to click the Send Now button. You connect to CompuServe and the message travels to the recipient's mailbox.

- Another way is to use the Out-Basket. This is handy if you want to write a number of messages and send them all at once. Also, if you do not finish writing a message, you can store it in the Out-Basket and finish it later.

If you've been following along with the example in this lesson, you should still be in the Create Mail dialog box. If you want to send the message as it is, click the Send Now button. If you want to send it to the Out-Basket, click the Out-Basket button. The Out-Basket button stores your message so you can send it later.

Sending Mail from the Out-Basket

If you have mail in your Out-Basket that you want to send, follow these steps to send it:

1. Click the Out-Basket icon on the Ribbon. The Out Basket dialog box opens (see Figure 13.5).

2. (Optional) If you want to edit a message, double-click on its name. The Create Mail dialog box appears again with the message in it. Edit the message, then click the Out-Basket button to close the dialog box.

3. Click one of the following buttons:

    - **Send** You connect to CompuServe and CompuServe sends the message.

- **Send All** You connect to CompuServe and CompuServe sends every message in your Out-Basket.

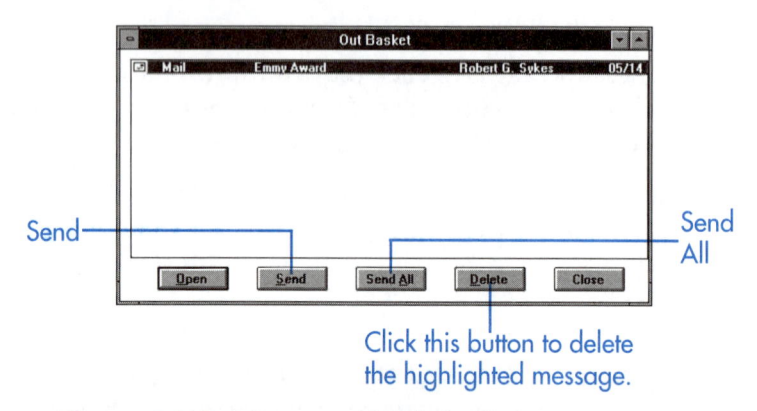

Figure 13.5 The Out Basket dialog box.

In this lesson, you learned how to create and send mail and how to use the Out-Basket. In the next lesson, you will learn how to receive your mail.

Lesson 14

Receiving Mail

In this lesson, you'll learn how to receive e-mail via CompuServe and store it in your In-Basket.

Using CompuServe's Mail System

It's an exciting event the first time you go online with CompuServe and see the Get New Mail icon on the Ribbon (see Figure 14.1). This means one or more electronic mail messages or files are waiting for you. The mail or files are currently in CompuServe's system. You can either read your mail online, or download it to your computer and read it offline.

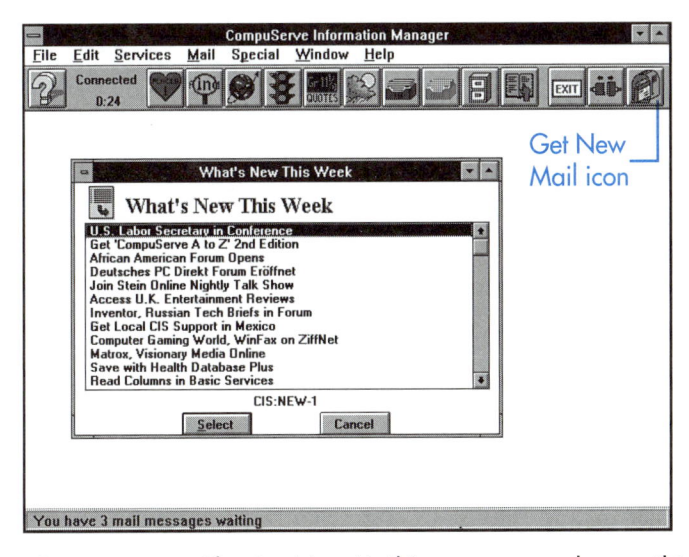

Figure 14.1 The Get New Mail icon appears when mail is waiting for you.

Lesson 14

> **Mail Call!** You'll only see the Get New Mail icon when you connect to CompuServe and you have new mail waiting.

Getting Your Mail

Unless you get a lot of "junk e-mail"—and want to delete some messages online—you will probably want to download all messages to your computer and read them offline.

Follow these steps to download all your mail:

1. Click the Get New Mail icon. The Get New Mail dialog box appears, listing the subjects of the messages and the sender's names (see Figure 14.2).

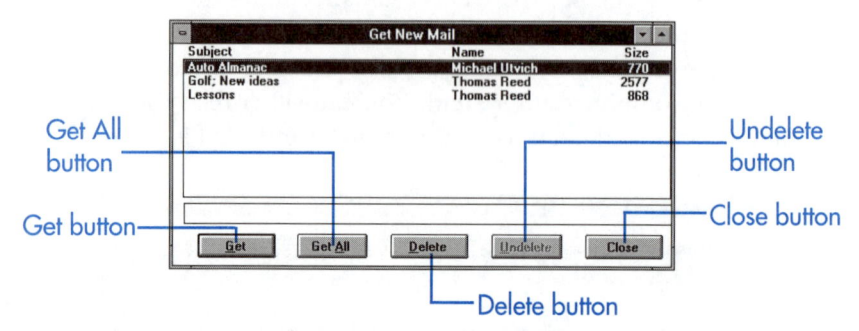

Figure 14.2 The Get New Mail dialog box routes new mail.

2. Click the Get All button. A message along the bottom of the dialog box tells you when your computer receives the messages.

3. Click the Disconnect icon to go offline.

Using the Get New Mail Dialog Box

It's important to understand the difference between the options in the Get New Mail dialog box. Otherwise, you may misplace your mail. The uses of the main buttons are:

Receiving Mail

- **Get**   Displays the highlighted message but *does not* put it in your In-Basket.

- **Get All**   Moves all messages to your In-Basket and closes the dialog box.

- **Delete**   Removes the highlighted message from your mail box.

- **Undelete**   Restores messages you have deleted.

> **Lost Mail**   It's very easy to confuse the uses of the Get and Get All buttons. Remember, Get displays the highlighted message; Get All moves the messages to your In-Basket.

Reading Mail Offline

Once all your messages are safely in your In-Basket and you disconnect from CompuServe, it's time to read your mail. At the main WinCIM desktop, follow these steps:

1. Click the In-Basket icon on the Ribbon. The In Basket dialog box opens (see Figure 14.3). The messages you just received are at the top of the list.

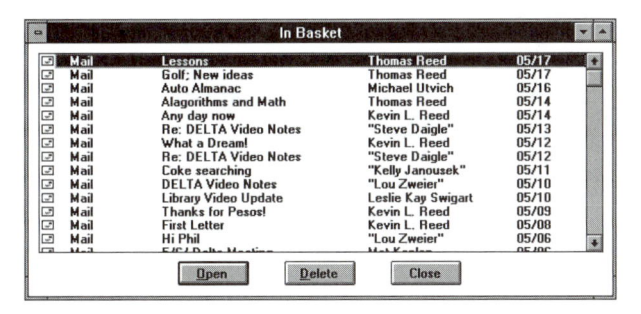

Figure 14.3   The most recent messages are at the top of the In-Basket.

2. Double-click the top message to view it. The text of the message appears.

3. Click the Next button to read the next message you just received.

4. Continue clicking Next until you have read all your messages.

> **File—What?** The presence of the File It button below the mail messages is confusing. It implies you may lose the message unless you file it. Here, File It means to actually file it in another location.

Managing Your In-Basket with the File It Button

You can store e-mail messages in your In-Basket indefinitely. CompuServe adds new messages to the top of the list. However, you may decide to file messages in a new folder in your Filing Cabinet instead of leaving them in your In-Basket. For this, you can use the File It button.

Follow these steps to create a new folder for mail in your Filing Cabinet and transfer an e-mail message into it:

1. Click the File It button. The Store Message dialog box appears. The Move option appears selected and the Store button is active.

2. Click the New button. The Add New Folder dialog box opens with the cursor in a blank space for the folder name.

3. Type in a name for your new folder, such as **MAIL**.

4. Click the OK button. The Add New Folder dialog box closes, and you return to the Store Message dialog box.

Receiving Mail

5. Click the Store button. CompuServe stores the message in the MAIL folder (if that's what you named in step 3), and the dialog box closes.

For instructions on how to retrieve the message from your Filing Cabinet, see Lesson 7.

E-Mail File Names If you want to open an e-mail message with your word processor, you may have a difficult time finding it. CompuServe stores messages in separate files with names, such as 2dd88315.plx. Unless you can crack the code, the best way to locate e-mail files is by the sequence they appear. The top message in your In-Basket will be the last message in the In-Basket subdirectory.

Copy and Paste E-Mail To quickly transfer the text of an e-mail message to your word processor, use the Copy and Paste features available in the e-mail dialog boxes. Select the text you want to copy and press Ctrl+C. Move to your word processor, and insert the text by pressing Ctrl+V.

Automating Your Mail

If you send and receive lots of e-mail, automate this process with the Send/Receive All Mail command under the Mail menu. When you choose this option, CompuServe sends all the stored mail in your Out-Basket and retrieves your new mail.

Disconnect When Done When using the Send/Receive All Mail command, you can tell WinCIM to disconnect automatically when it has accomplished this task. Click on Send/Receive All Mail on the Mail menu. In the Send and Receive

All Mail dialog box, click on the box next to **Disconnect when Done**. An **X** appears to indicate the selected feature.

In this lesson, you learned how to get your mail, store it in your In-Basket, and move it to your Filing Cabinet. In Lesson 15, you will learn how to use the CompuServe mail system to send files.

Lesson 15

Sending Files

In this lesson, you'll learn how to send a file to another CompuServe member via the online mail system.

Using the Send Files Option

At times, sending a computer file to another person is more convenient than shipping hard copies by express mail, faxing the document, or sending the file by modem. Here are several advantages to sending files through CompuServe:

- The files arrive almost instantly.
- CompuServe loads the files into the recipient's computer system.
- The recipient can download the files at his convenience.
- You can condense files (*zip* them) to save transfer costs.

> **Plain English**
>
> **Zipping a File** To save a file in a condensed format. You can zip and unzip with utility programs, such as PKZIP and PKUNZIP. You can download these programs from many CompuServe forums (see Lesson 19).

When to Send Files

When you send e-mail messages, you are sending small files. So why is there a separate Send File command on the Mail menu on the command bar? (See Figure 15.1.)

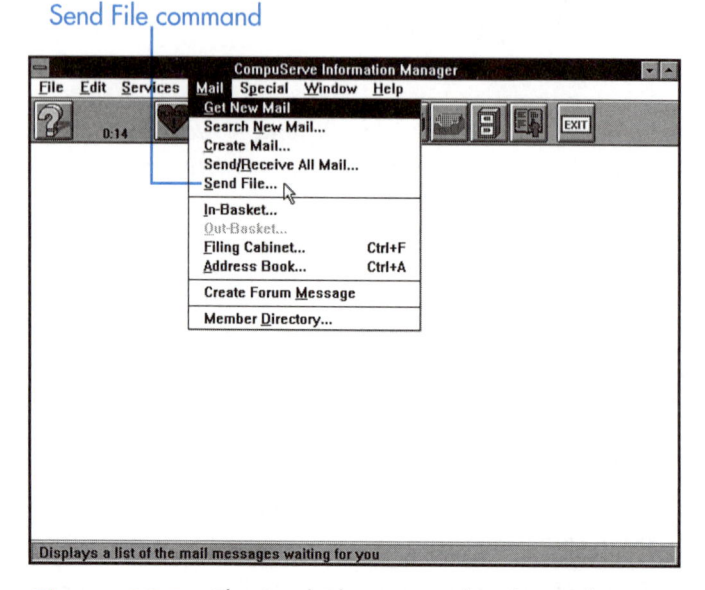

Figure 15.1 The Send File command in the Mail menu.

Choose Send File when you want to send:

- Text files created by other programs such as WordPerfect.

- Spreadsheets created by programs, such as Lotus 1-2-3.

- Long files or group of files that you have zipped.

- Graphics or sound files.

What Does It Cost?

Sending text files is comparable to the cost of a long-distance fax. However, it's much cheaper than sending hard copies by express mail. For example, a four-page text document created in Word for Windows costs about $.70 to send via CompuServe. It takes about 45 seconds to transmit (depending on your modem's baud rate). Sending graphics files is usually more expensive. Even a single graphic file, a photograph for example, can cost about $3 to send over CompuServe. CompuServe will tell you exactly how much it will cost before you send any files.

Getting Ready to Send a File

The process of sending a file is similar to sending mail. However, there are some subtle—and important—differences.

Follow these steps to send a file via CompuServe:

1. Click Mail on the menu bar. The Mail menu appears.

2. Click Send File. The Recipient List and Send File Message dialog boxes appear, one in front of the other (see Figure 15.2).

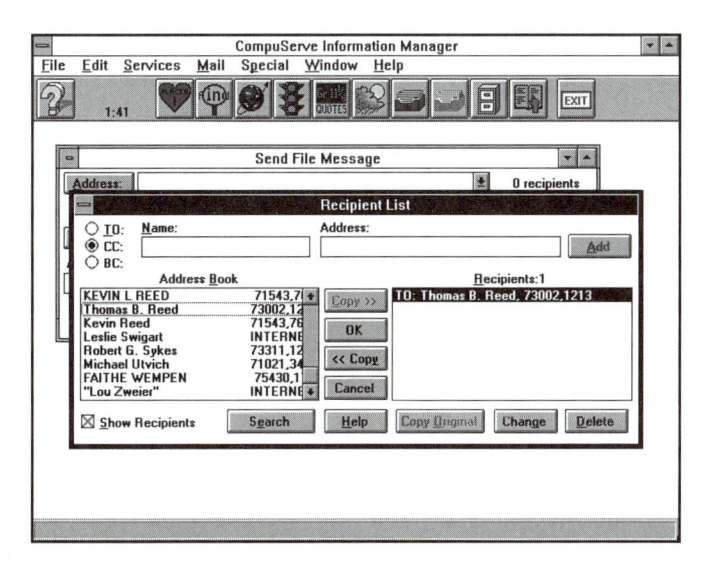

Figure 15.2 The Recipient List and Send File Message dialog boxes.

3. Select the person you want to send the file to by moving the mouse pointer over his or her name in the Address Book. (You can also type in the name and address of anyone who isn't in the Address Book.)

4. Click the Copy >> button, or press Enter. The person's name and address appear in the right-hand box labeled Recipients.

5. (Optional) Click other names, and copy them to the Recipients list.

6. Click OK or press Enter. The Recipient List dialog box closes, and the Send File Message dialog box is visible.

7. Type in a subject for the file (the Send Now button won't become active until you do this).

8. Click the File button. The Open dialog box appears (see Figure 15.3).

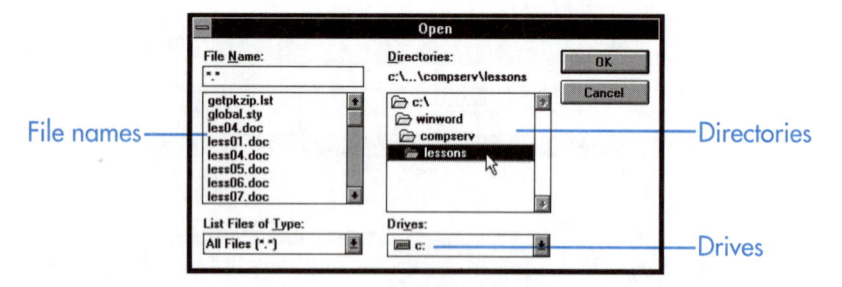

Figure 15.3 The Open dialog box inserts the name of the file to send.

9. Highlight the file you want to send by changing directories and scrolling through the files.

10. Double-click the file you want to send. The Open box closes, and you return to the Send File Message dialog box (see Figure 15.4).

Sending Files 93

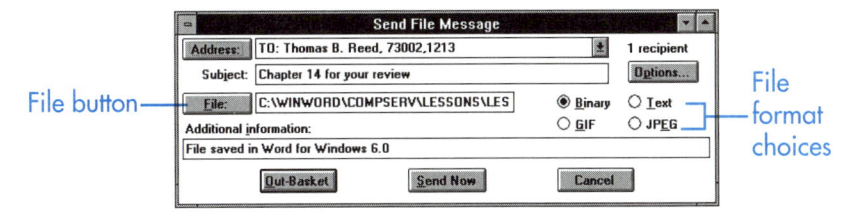

Figure 15.4 The Send File Message dialog box.

(File button points to the **File:** button; File format choices point to Binary / Text / GIF / JPEG radio buttons.)

Choosing a File Format

In the Send File Message dialog box, there are four choices for the file you are transmitting. These are:

- **Binary**   Use this for sending executable programs or files created by a word processor.

- **Text**   You can send files saved in ASCII format using this option. However, you may lose formatting commands (margins, tabs, and indents) in the file.

- **GIF**   Use this option to identify Graphics Interchange format files.

- **JPEG**   Use this option to identify Journalists Photographic Expert Group files.

Binary is the default choice because it has the broadest application.

Sending a File

You have made all the selections and are ready to send the file. If you have several files in the Out-Basket that you want to send, you can send them all at once. To send files from the Out-Basket see Lesson 13.

If you have just one file to send, first select it, and then follow these steps:

1. Click the Send Now button. You connect to CompuServe, and CompuServe sends the file.

2. (Optional) If a dialog box appears notifying you of a transaction charge for sending the file, click OK to approve the extra charge and send the file.

3. Click the Disconnect icon when the transmission is complete.

> **Automatic Disconnect** Sometimes, sending a file can take a long time. Don't sit and watch the screen to find out when to disconnect. Instead, put the file in your Out-Basket, and then choose the "Disconnect When Done" option (see Lesson 13).

You can simplify the process of sending multiple files by zipping them together into a single, smaller file. This also reduces the cost. Find out how to get PKZIP and PKUNZIP (the programs you use to zip and unzip files) from CompuServe in Lesson 20. See Appendix D for an explanation of their use.

In this lesson, you learned how to send a file via CompuServe's mail system. In the next lesson, you will learn how to receive a file from someone else.

Lesson 16

Receiving Files

In this lesson, you'll learn how to download a file that someone sends to you through the CompuServe mail system.

Moving Files from CompuServe into Your System

Receiving a file is easier than sending one. In fact, you may download a file without even realizing that's what you're doing. That's because the person sending it to you chooses most of the options (the same options you learned how to set in Lesson 15). However, you still have to make sure to download it properly and that you can find it once you are offline.

As you learned in Lesson 14, when someone sends a file to you, the Get New Mail icon appears on the Ribbon (see Figure 16.1). However, you can't tell at this point whether you are receiving an e-mail message or a file. As you proceed, CompuServe will tell you a *file* is waiting for you to download, and you can choose a place in which to store it.

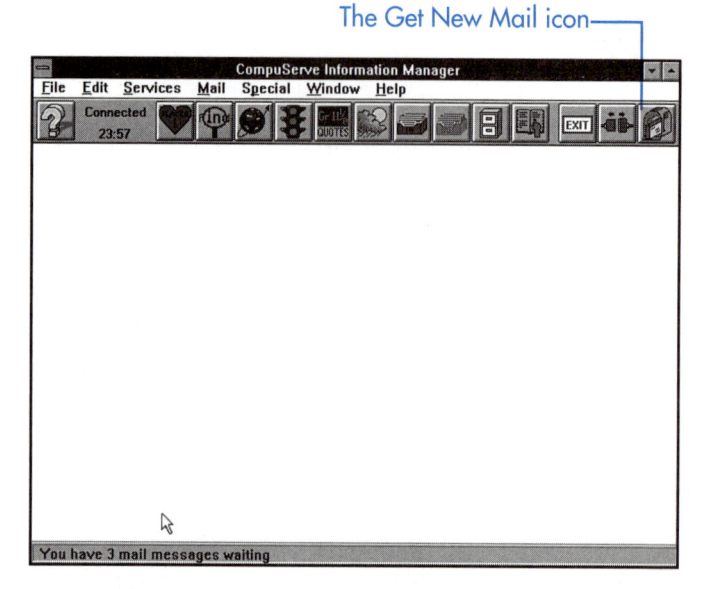

Figure 16.1 The Get New Mail icon can mean a file is waiting for you.

Getting a File

If you are online and the Get New Mail icon is on the Ribbon, follow these steps to get a file from your mail box:

1. Click the Get New Mail icon. The Get New Mail dialog box appears. It lists the new messages and their subjects (see Figure 16.2).

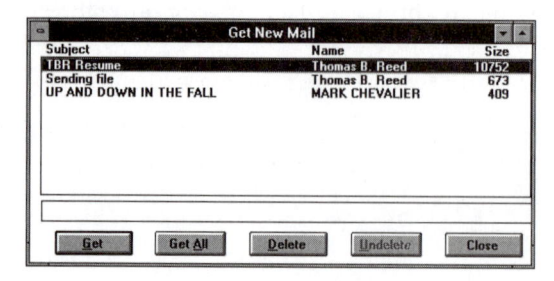

Figure 16.2 The Get New Mail dialog box.

Receiving Files 97

2. Click the Get All button. A box appears with a bar graph to show the progress of the downloading.

3. After the computer downloads the file, click the Disconnect icon to go offline. CompuServe stores the downloaded files and messages in your In-Basket.

4. Click the In Basket icon. The new messages appear at the top of the list.

5. Scroll through the messages using the Next button (see Lesson 13). You will reach a message that tells you that your computer has received a file (see Figure 16.3).

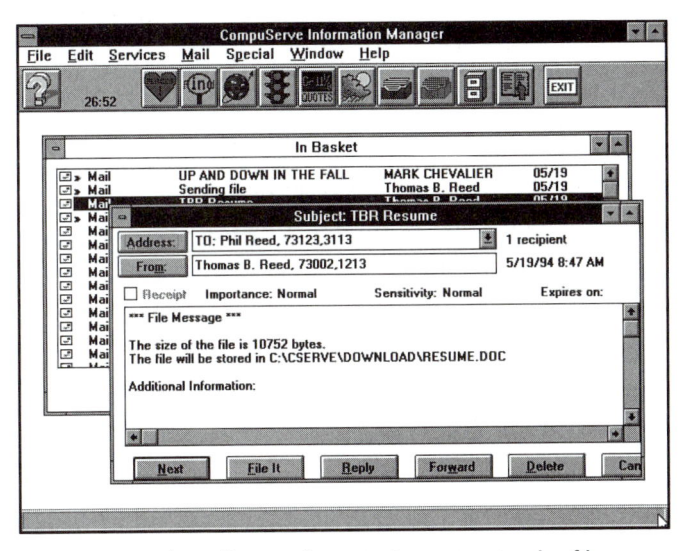

Figure 16.3 This tells you that you have received a file.

You can now rest assured that CompuServe safely downloaded the file to your system. The next step is finding it and opening it.

Finding and Moving a File

CompuServe automatically places the files you receive in the **DOWNLOAD** suddirectory. However, if it is a word processor document or a spreadsheet file, you will want to move the file to that application before you open it. To do that, use File Manager in Windows.

To move the file you just downloaded from CompuServe, follow these steps:

1. Go to Program Manager by doing one of the following:

   - Hold down the Alt key and press the Tab key. A small box with the name of an open application will appear in the middle of your screen. Keep holding down the Alt key, and press the Tab key to cycle through all open applications. When you reach Program Manager, release the Alt key.

   - Close WinCIM by clicking the Exit icon on the Ribbon or by selecting the File Exit command.

   - Minimize WinCIM by clicking the Minimize button in the upper right corner.

2. From the Program Manager window, open the Main program group.

3. Double-click the File Manager icon. The File Manager main screen appears (Figure 16.4).

4. Click the CSERVE directory in the left box. The CSERVE subdirectories appear in the right box.

5. Click the DOWNLOAD subdirectory. The files appear.

6. Highlight the file you want to move by clicking on it.

Receiving Files

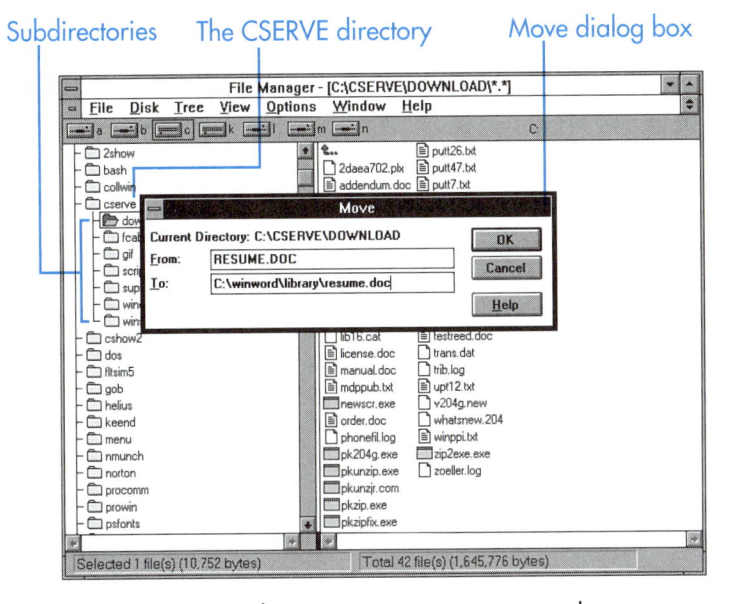

Figure 16.4 File Manager's Move command.

7. Click File on the menu bar. A pull-down menu opens.

8. Click Move. The Move dialog box opens.

9. Type in the name and location of the file.

10. Click OK. The file disappears from the DOWNLOAD subdirectory.

11. Double-click the Close button in File Manager.

> **Save As** You may prefer to use the Save As command found in the File menu of most Windows-based programs to copy a file to a different subdirectory. While running your application, open the file from the DOWNLOAD subdirectory in CSERVE. Then use File Save As to store it in its new location. But remember, you now have two copies of the same file.

After loading another program, you can now open the file you received through the CompuServe mail system.

In this lesson, you learned how to download a file from the mail system, and then how to move that file to another directory. In the next lesson, you will learn about CompuServe's link to the Internet.

Lesson 17

Using the Internet

In this lesson, you will learn how to send and receive e-mail through the Internet and about the Internet Forum.

Getting Ready for the Internet

There's a lot of talk these days about the Internet and the information superhighway. While the wonders of the Internet have captured the public's imagination, it remains difficult to use. At the time of this writing, CompuServe intends to provide full access to the Internet. CompuServe plans to design WinCIM to make accessing the Internet more friendly.

Even now, CompuServe provides several Internet-related services. You can send and receive e-mail via the Internet, and you can participate in CompuServe's Internet Forum.

What Is the Internet?

The Internet is an electronic mail system connecting governmental institutions, military branches, educational institutions, and commercial companies. On the Internet you can also search for and retrieve information from thousands of separate databases worldwide.

Sending E-Mail on the Internet

Using CompuServe to send e-mail to someone on the Internet isn't difficult, but it requires a slightly different addressing format. For this example, we'll assume your friend John Stevens has given you his e-mail address as J_STEVENS@NEZ.COM.

To send an e-mail message to John Stevens, follow these steps:

1. Click Mail on the menu bar. The Mail pull-down menu appears.

2. Click Create Mail. The Recipient List dialog box appears with the cursor in the Name text box.

3. Enter the recipient's name. In this case, you would type John Stevens.

4. Click the Address Box.

5. Enter the recipient's address. You have to type **INTERNET:** first, and then the person's address. In this case, you would type INTERNET:J_STEVENS@NEZ.COM (see Figure 17.1).

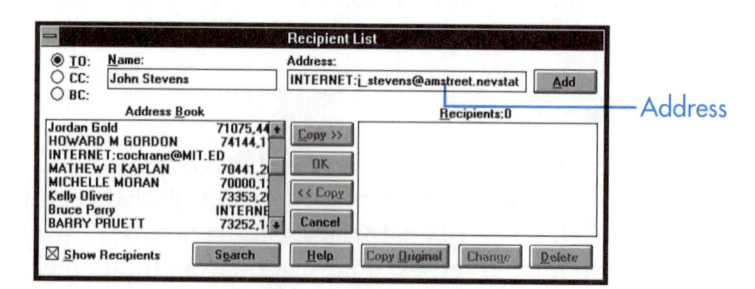

Figure 17.1 INTERNET: precedes the address in the Address box.

6. Click the Add button. CompuServe adds the name and address to the Recipients List.

Using the Internet

7. (Optional) Click the Copy button to add this name and address to your Address Book. When the Add to Address Book dialog box opens, click OK.

8. In the Recipient List dialog box, click OK. The Create Mail box appears.

From this point on, the process is identical to sending e-mail to another CompuServe member. Follow the steps in Lesson 13 to finish sending the message.

> **Wrong Address** If the e-mail format is incorrect, and CompuServe is unable to send the message, you receive a note in your In-Basket—assuming you are using the Send/Receive All Mail option (see Figure 17.2). If the Internet address does not exist, you will soon receive a message notifying you of undelivered mail. You can then attempt to correct the problem and resend the message.

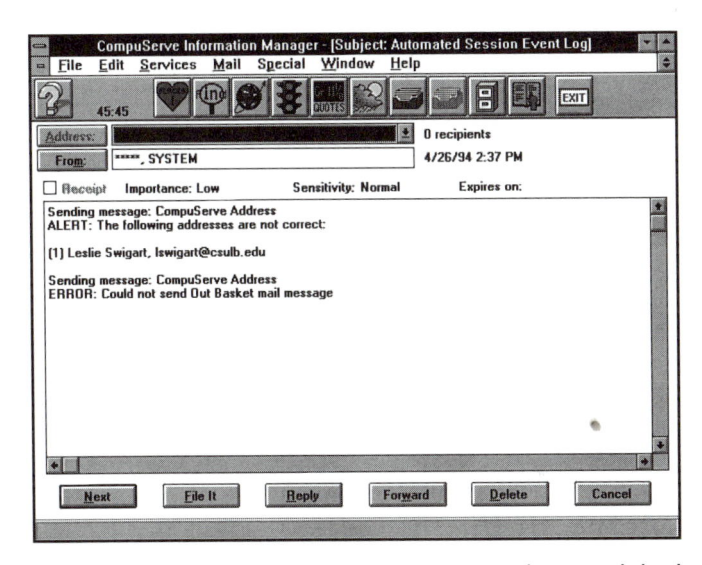

Figure 17.2 This message means you used an invalid adress format.

Receiving E-Mail on the Internet

To receive e-mail on the Internet you don't have to do anything special. However, CompuServe charges you for this service. The rates are .15 cents for the first 7,500 characters and .05 cents for each additional 2,500 characters.

Since CompuServe charges you for receiving mail via the Internet, you will see a message in your In-Basket when you use the Send/Receive All Mail selection (see Figure 17.3).

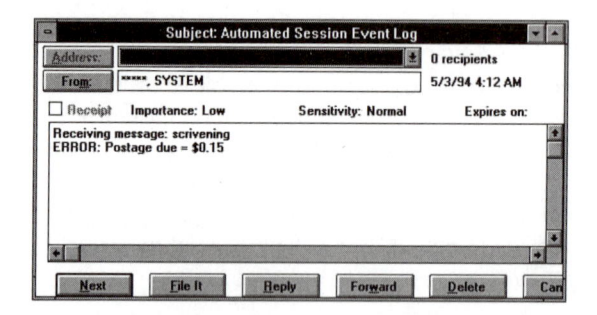

Figure 17.3 When you receive Internet mail, this message appears in your In-Basket.

Get—Nothing You cannot retrieve mail that comes via the Internet by using the Disconnect When Done setting in the Send/Receive All Mail dialog box. If you try, a system error message appears in your mail box saying there is postage due. Instead of doing that, click the Get New Mail icon, and then click Get. The message appears, and you can click the In-Basket button to save it.

Accept All Mail You can change your settings so WinCIM will always accept all mail, even if there is postage due on it. Click Special on the menu bar, and then choose Preferences. Click Mail to open the Mail Preferences dialog box. Now click the Always retrieve option button under the Postage Due Messages section.

Your Internet Address

Your CompuServe ID number is, in a sense, an Internet address. Anyone with access to the Internet can send you a message this way: list your CompuServe ID number, and then @compuserve.com. The full address looks like this: **73123,3113@compuserve.com**.

The Internet Forum

While CompuServe is not yet an Internet gateway, there is valuable information here that can lead you to the information superhighway. You can find this information in the Internet Forum. (See Lessons 19 and 20 to learn about Forums.)

The Internet Forum contains:

- Tips on navigating the Internet.
- Internet access numbers across the country.
- Information about Internet software.
- Addresses of Internet bulletin boards and databases.

GO Internet Forum If you can't wait to get started learning about the Internet, click the Go icon, and enter INETFORUM. From here, check the Library section called "Getting Started" (see Figure 17.4).

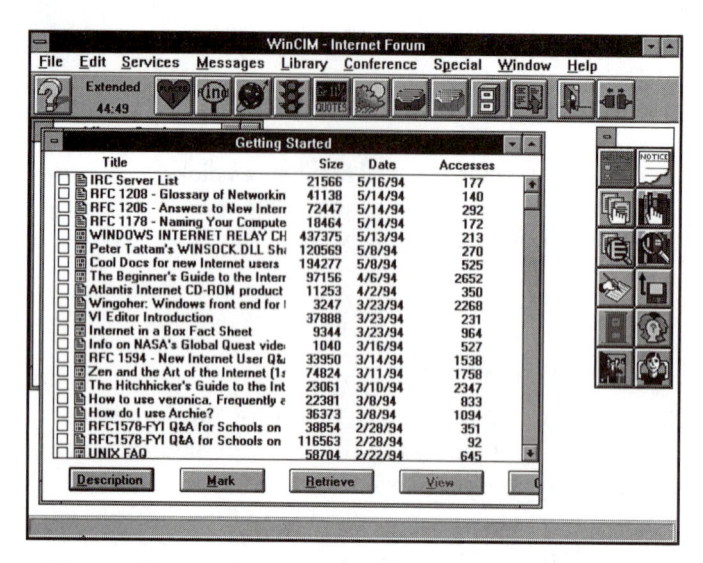

Figure 17.4 The Getting Started Library section of the Internet Forum covers many topics.

In this lesson, you learned how to address e-mail to send over the Internet and how to reach the Internet Forum. In the next lesson, you will learn how to go shopping in The Electronic Mall.

Lesson 18

Online Shopping

In this lesson, you will learn how to browse a store in The Electronic Mall and search for a specific product.

Shopping Unlimited

The phrase "shop till you drop" loses meaning with online shopping. There's no way to get tired browsing in this mall. All you have to do to change stores is move your mouse pointer and click.

CompuServe's basic service includes unlimited free access to The Electronic Mall. The interface has been recently renovated to be more compatible with WinCIM, and CompuServe continues to add more retailers. Some stores feature graphics of available products.

The Electronic Mall offers these advantages over an actual mall:

- It's open 24-hours a day.
- You can reduce commuting time to zero.
- You can quickly search for hard-to-find products.
- The stores process your orders quickly.
- You don't have to deal with sore feet or cranky kids.

Even if you're a confirmed "hands-on" shopper, you should take a moment to visit The Electronic Mall.

Just Browsing

There are two ways to browse in The Electronic Mall on CompuServe. You can shop by:

- **Department**   This gives you a listing of general groups of products (clothing, sporting goods, and so on) and where you can find them.

- **Merchant**   CompuServe provides an alphabetical listing of all the retailers in the Electronic Mall.

In the example in this lesson, you'll use the Merchant listing to find your favorite retailer.

Entering the Mall

Before you can start shopping, you have to get to the mall. That's never been easier than with CompuServe. Just follow these steps:

> **GO MALL**   Take the express route to the mall. Click on the Go icon on the ribbon, and then enter MALL. You connect to CompuServe and go directly to The Electronic Mall's opening menu.

1. In the Services window, click the Shopping icon.

2. In The Electronic Mall/Shopping dialog box, double-click on The Electronic MALL.

3. You connect to the CompuServe network (if you aren't already) and proceed to an Alert window labeled MALL. Click Proceed to go to the next window.

4. The Electronic Mall dialog box appears, with the ENTER ELECTRONIC MALL entry highlighted (see Figure 18.1).

Online Shopping

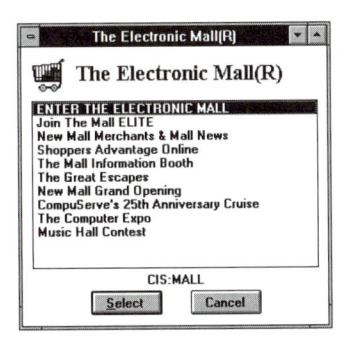

```
┌─────────────────────────────────┐
│     The Electronic Mall(R)      │
├─────────────────────────────────┤
│  🛒  The Electronic Mall(R)     │
│  ┌───────────────────────────┐  │
│  │ ENTER THE ELECTRONIC MALL │  │
│  │ Join The Mall ELITE       │  │
│  │ New Mall Merchants & Mall News │
│  │ Shoppers Advantage Online │  │
│  │ The Mall Information Booth│  │
│  │ The Great Escapes         │  │
│  │ New Mall Grand Opening    │  │
│  │ CompuServe's 25th Anniversary Cruise │
│  │ The Computer Expo         │  │
│  │ Music Hall Contest        │  │
│  └───────────────────────────┘  │
│           CIS:MALL              │
│      [ Select ]  [ Cancel ]     │
└─────────────────────────────────┘
```

Figure 18.1 This screen provides access to The Electronic Mall.

5. Click the Select button or press Enter. You enter the Mall and a box opens called Mall Directory of Merchants.

Using Merchant QuickSearch

To find a retailer, follow these steps, with Hammacher Schlemmer as an example. (If you want to see if your favorite store is online, use these instructions and substitute its name.):

1. Double-click on Shop by Merchant. A dialog box opens.

2. Enter list in the text box, or type the first few letters of the merchant you're looking for (in this case, HAM), then press Enter. An alphabetical listing appears.

3. Scroll down to the merchant you want, in this case, Hammacher Schlemmer.

4. Double-click on the merchant. (Double-click Hammacher Schlemmer for the example.) The Alert window appears to notify you that you are about to enter the store.

Lesson 18

5. Click Proceed or press Enter. You enter the store and the main window appears. For this example, the main window is Hammacher Schlemmer with **SHOP OUR ONLINE STORE** highlighted (see Figure 18.2).

```
                 HAMMACHER SCHLEMMER
           HAMMACHER SCHLEMMER
    SHOP OUR ONLINE STORE
    Product "QuickSearch"
    ORDERING and SHIPPING Information
    "Our Unconditional Guarantee"
    Retail LOCATIONS
    Request Our FREE Full-Color CATALOG
    Order From Our Print CATALOG
    JOIN Our Electronic Mailing List
    GIFT CERTIFICATE / CORPORATE GIFTS


                [ Select ]        [ Cancel ]
```

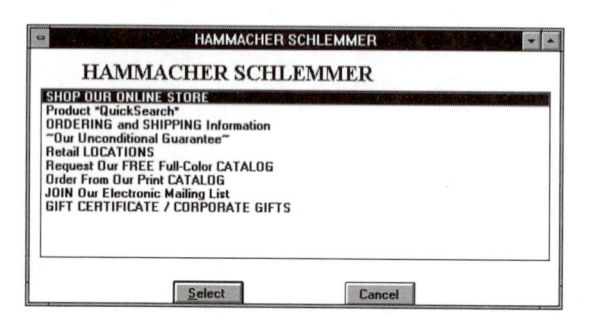

Figure 18.2 The introductory window of a Mall store.

6. Double-click the highlighted choice, or press Enter. You are now in the store.

> **Express Route** The stores in The Electronic Mall all have quick reference words, such as HS for Hammacher Schlemmer. Click the GO icon, enter HS and you land directly in the store's opening screen. These quick reference words appear in brackets beside the merchant listing in the above Step 4.

Once you are inside the store, it's time to choose your department so you can see the offered products.

Choosing a Department and a Product

You are getting close to the actual products now. All you have to do is choose a department. To find and enter a department, follow these steps:

Online Shopping   **111**

1. Scroll down the list of departments, and double-click on the department, or press Enter. A new window appears with the name of the department at the top (see Figure 18.3).

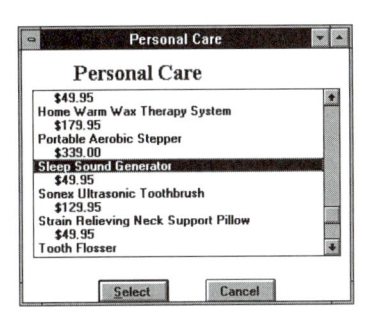

```
┌─ Personal Care ──────────┐
│      Personal Care       │
│  $49.95                  │
│  Home Warm Wax Therapy System │
│  $179.95                 │
│  Portable Aerobic Stepper│
│  $339.00                 │
│  Sleep Sound Generator   │
│  $49.95                  │
│  Sonex Ultrasonic Toothbrush │
│  $129.95                 │
│  Strain Relieving Neck Support Pillow │
│  $49.95                  │
│  Tooth Flosser           │
│     [Select]  [Cancel]   │
└──────────────────────────┘
```

Figure 18.3 This is a department of a Mall store, displaying its products.

2. Scroll through the list. When you see something interesting, double-click on the product, or press Enter. A new screen appears with product details and ordering buttons (see Figure 18.4).

3. Click the Prev Item button or Next Item button to continue browsing in this department.

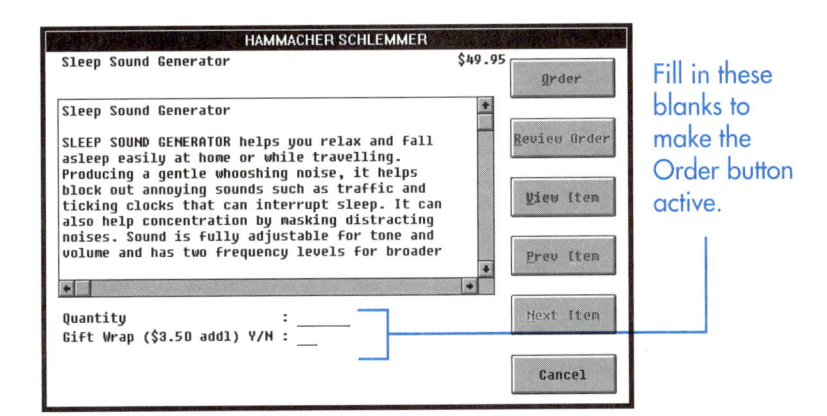

```
┌─ HAMMACHER SCHLEMMER ──────────────────┐
│ Sleep Sound Generator        $49.95    │
│                              [ Order ] │
│ Sleep Sound Generator                  │
│                              [Review Order] │
│ SLEEP SOUND GENERATOR helps you relax and fall │
│ asleep easily at home or while travelling. │
│ Producing a gentle whooshing noise, it helps │
│ block out annoying sounds such as traffic and │[View Item]
│ ticking clocks that can interrupt sleep. It can │
│ also help concentration by masking distracting │
│ noises. Sound is fully adjustable for tone and │
│ volume and has two frequency levels for broader │[Prev Item]
│                                        │
│ Quantity            : ____             │
│ Gift Wrap ($3.50 addl) Y/N : __        │[Next Item]
│                                        │
│                              [ Cancel ]│
└────────────────────────────────────────┘
```

Fill in these blanks to make the Order button active.

Figure 18.4 This screen displays product information and begins the ordering process.

Order, Order If you want to buy something that you see, but can't get the Order button to become active, make sure you have filled in all the blanks (see Figure 18.4).

Using Product QuickSearch

At times, you may not want to browse. You may want to find a specific item within a store. For this, you can use QuickSearch and locate the item using a key word.

To use QuickSearch, follow these steps:

1. Go to the store's main screen. (If you are following along with the example in this lesson, click the Cancel button in each of the three dialog boxes to return to the main screen.)

2. Double-click Product *QuickSearch*. The QuickSearch dialog box appears (see Figure 18.5).

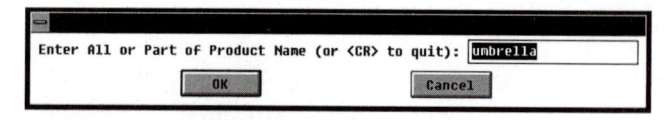

```
Enter All or Part of Product Name (or <CR> to quit): umbrella
              OK                          Cancel
```

Figure 18.5 The QuickSearch dialog box.

3. Enter the name of the product or a key word.

4. Click OK or press Enter. The result of the search appears in the Product QuickSearch dialog box.

5. (Optional) Double-click the product name to get more information and to order it.

6. If you're ready to exit the Mall, do so by clicking on the Disconnect icon on the Ribbon.

While The Electronic Mall may not currently satisfy your shopping urge, keep your eye on it as it becomes bigger and more sophisticated.

In this lesson, you learned to enter The Electronic Mall, browse a store, and search for a specific item. In the next lesson, you will learn how to use CompuServe to make travel arrangements.

Lesson 19

Making Travel Plans

In this lesson, you will learn how to use CompuServe to locate airline flights and check the ticket prices.

Using EAASY SABRE (CIM)

When making travel plans, it would be convenient to have a list of all airline flights from one city to another. It would also be nice to be able to check fares and restrictions on these flights—without testing the patience of a travel agent.

A special service on CompuServe, EAASY SABRE, makes travel planning a breeze. CompuServe revamped EAASY SABRE for WinCIM and is more friendly than earlier DOS versions.

If you are a frequent flier, you will eventually want to join AAdvantage. This service, provided by American Airlines, costs nothing extra and gives you special privileges for booking flights. For now, however, we're just going to browse for flights and low fares on EAASY SABRE (CIM).

Accessing EAASY SABRE (CIM)

From the WinCIM desktop, follow these steps to enter EAASY SABRE (CIM):

GO SABRECIM Before planning your route, try taking a shortcut to EAASY SABRE (CIM). Click on the Go icon on the ribbon, and then type **SABRECIM**. You connect to CompuServe and go directly to EAASY SABRE (CIM).

Making Travel Plans 115

1. In the Services group window, click the Travel icon. You connect to CompuServe, and the Travel window opens.

2. Double-click Air/Hotel/Car Information. The Basic Air/Hotel/Car Information window opens.

3. Double-click EAASY SABRE (CIM). The EAASY SABRE window opens.

4. Double-click Access EAASY SABRE (CIM). A Welcome screen appears.

5. Click the Browse button. An untitled EAASY SABRE (CIM) menu appears with Flights & Fares highlighted.

6. Double-click Flights & Fares. The Destination dialog box opens (see Figure 19.1). The cursor is in the blank for Departure City or Code. Notice the Flights button is not active yet.

Enter the city name here; the code will be filled in later.

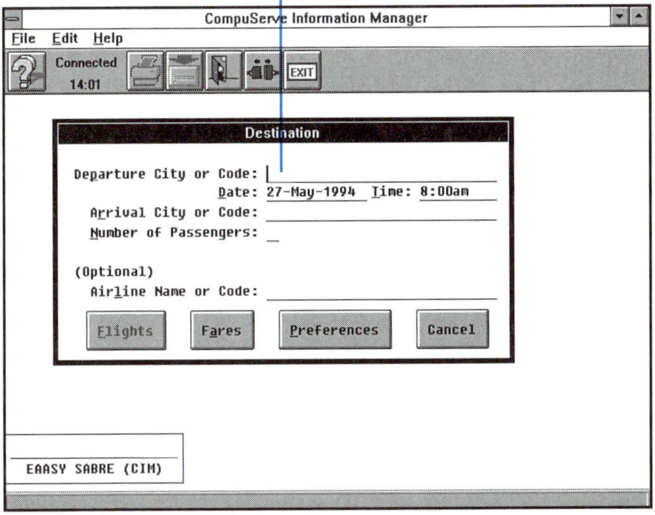

Figure 19.1 Provide flight details in the Destination dialog box.

Lesson 19

City Code? Unless you're a ticket agent, you probably don't know the code of the city you're flying to. Don't worry. Just type in the name of the city (the code appears later).

7. Enter the city you plan to depart from.

8. (Optional) Change the date if you are planning to leave on a day that's different from the one shown on-screen.

9. Click Arrival City or Code.

10. Enter your destination under Arrival City or Code.

11. Click Number of Passengers.

12. Enter the number of passengers. Notice that the Flights button is now active.

13. (Optional) Click Airline Name or Code, and then enter the airline you prefer to travel on. If you leave this blank, EAASY SABRE (CIM) searches all airlines.

14. Click the Flights button. The Select Airport dialog box appears (see Figure 19.2).

```
           Select Airport
  Code   Airport

  LAX   LOS ANGELES, CA
  LSQ   LOS ANGELES, CHILE



       [  OK  ]    [ Cancel ]
```

Figure 19.2 This dialog box confirms city choice to input airport code.

Making Travel Plans

15. Click OK if the highlighted selection is correct. Or make a different choice, and click OK. A similar dialog box appears.

16. Click OK if the highlighted selection is correct. Or make a different choice, and click OK. A Flights For dialog box appears listing all flights that match the information you provided (see Figure 19.3).

```
                        Flights for
              LOS ANGELES, CA to WASHINGTON, DC
                      Fri 27-May-1994
    Type      Departure    Arrival   Airline    Stops Plane

    Direct    LAX 11:15A BWI  7:10P   US@         0    734
    Direct    LAX 11:40A IAD  7:21P   UA@         0    757
    Direct    LAX  1:15P IAD  8:52P   UA@         0    D10
    Direct    LAX  1:30P IAD  9:08P   AA@         0    D10
    Direct    LAX  1:30P IAD  9:08P   QF@         0    D10
    Direct    LAX  9:55P IAD  5:34A   UA@         0    757

                  @ = FAST Confirmation Segment

        [ Select ]   [ Detail ]   [ Fares ]   [ Cancel ]
```

Begins an itinerary — Select

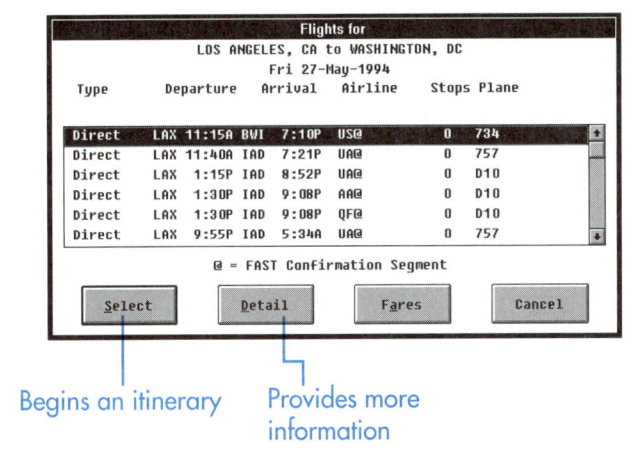

Provides more information — Detail

Figure 19.3 All flights between the two cities appear in this window.

Checking Fares

Once you find a flight that satisfies your time requirements, you probably want to know the fare and if there are any restrictions. To check fares and restrictions, follow these steps:

1. Highlight the flight you want to see the fare for.

2. Click the Fares button. The Published Fares For dialog box appears listing all the fares and some restrictions (see Figure 19.4).

Lesson 19

```
                Published Fares for
          LOS ANGELES, CA to WASHINGTON, DC
                  Fri 27-May-1994
                   Airline: USAIR
                    Fares in USD
    One      Round    Fare      Advance     Stay
    Way      Trip     Basis     Purchase    Min/Max

   299.00              BN         No       No  /  No
   693.00              Y8         No       No  /  No
   843.00              F8         No       No  /  No
  1137.00              Y          No       No  /  No
  1706.00              F          No       No  /  No


  [Flights]   [Rules]   [Change Return Date]   [Cancel]
```

Figure 19.4 Fares and some restrictions appear in this dialog box.

3. Click the Rules button. A Fare Rules For screen opens.

4. Double-click All Rules. The restrictions appear for you to review (see Figure 19.5).

5. Return to the Flights For screen by clicking OK, and then clicking the Cancel button in the next two screens.

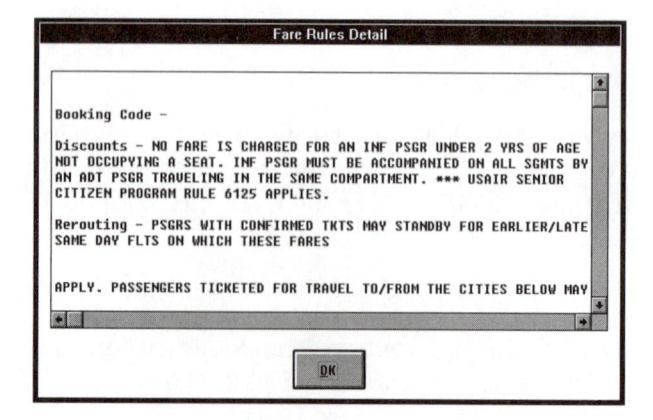

```
                    Fare Rules Detail

 Booking Code -

 Discounts - NO FARE IS CHARGED FOR AN INF PSGR UNDER 2 YRS OF AGE
 NOT OCCUPYING A SEAT. INF PSGR MUST BE ACCOMPANIED ON ALL SGMTS BY
 AN ADT PSGR TRAVELING IN THE SAME COMPARTMENT. *** USAIR SENIOR
 CITIZEN PROGRAM RULE 6125 APPLIES.

 Rerouting - PSGRS WITH CONFIRMED TKTS MAY STANDBY FOR EARLIER/LATE
 SAME DAY FLTS ON WHICH THESE FARES

 APPLY. PASSENGERS TICKETED FOR TRAVEL TO/FROM THE CITIES BELOW MAY

                          [OK]
```

Figure 19.5 Flight restrictions appear under All Rules.

Making Travel Plans 119

Visiting the Itinerary Feature

An advanced feature of EAASY SABRE (CIM), not fully covered here, is its capability to build an itinerary for you. Let's take a quick look at this feature before exiting.

To see the main Itinerary screen, click the Select button in the Flights for dialog box. An Itinerary screen opens (see Figure 19.6).

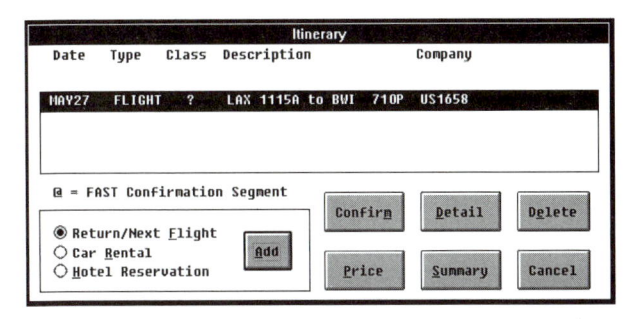

Figure 19.6 The Itinerary dialog box enables you to add car rental, hotel reservations, and other flights.

The buttons in the Itinerary dialog box enable you to do several things:

- **Add** or **Delete** buttons are for car rentals, hotel reservations, and additional flight segments.
- **Confirm** will book your reservations when you finish.
- **Price** supplies a running total of your entire travel expenses as you add or delete elements.
- **Detail** shows times, prices, meals, and other flight information.
- **Summary** displays all the elements of your plans on one screen.

Take Off Remember to go offline by clicking the Disconnect icon on the ribbon.

EAASY SABRE (CIM) is a powerful tool with many more features than were covered in this lesson. If you travel frequently, it would be worth investigating it further in the future.

In this lesson, you learned how to look up airline flights on EAASY SABRE (CIM) and check ticket prices. In the next lesson, you will learn about CompuServe Forums.

Lesson 20

Using Forums

In this lesson, you'll learn how to use the Forum Toolbox to search for a utility program and download it to your computer.

Understanding Forums

Maybe you're a wine connoisseur and you want to broaden your knowledge of Spanish vintages. Perhaps you're a news camera operator looking for a job. Or maybe it's the night before a big presentation and you need a graphics driver for your laptop.

You can find the solution to all these needs—and many more—in CompuServe forums. A *forum* is a special section of CompuServe, managed by a *Sysop*, where members with the same interest can meet to exchange information, files, and programs. There is a good chance that, whatever your profession or hobby, there is a forum on CompuServe devoted to that subject.

> **Sysop** *Sysop* stands for system operator. Sysops answer questions from members and generally guide the direction of the Forum.

Find Your Forum To find a forum that addresses your interest, use the Find icon (see Lesson 4) and search for a key word. Or just click on the Find icon and type in the word **Forum**. A list of CompuServe forums appear.

Convenience—At a Cost

Most of the forums in CompuServe are in extended services. You will pay $.16 a minute, plus connect charges, at 9600 and 14400 baud rate and $.08 for 300, 1200 and 2400 baud rates. To keep your expenses down, you should become efficient at navigating forums. If you linger to browse, you may forget time is passing and the cost is rising.

Forum Activities

There are several main activities in forums. You can:

- Search for and download shareware games, programs, and graphics.
- Search for messages on specific subjects.
- Post messages for other forum members.
- "Chat" with other members who are online at that moment.

To carry out all these different activities, CompuServe has designed a special Forum desktop element called a Toolbox.

Using the Forum Toolbox

There are several main areas in forums, all of which you can reach through the Toolbox (see Figure 20.1). The areas are:

- **Libraries** Files, programs, and graphics are stored here under different "Sections."

Using Forums 123

- **Message Sections**   Members use this area to exchange information. The subjects are also organized in "Sections."

- **Conference Rooms**   Online members "chat" here.

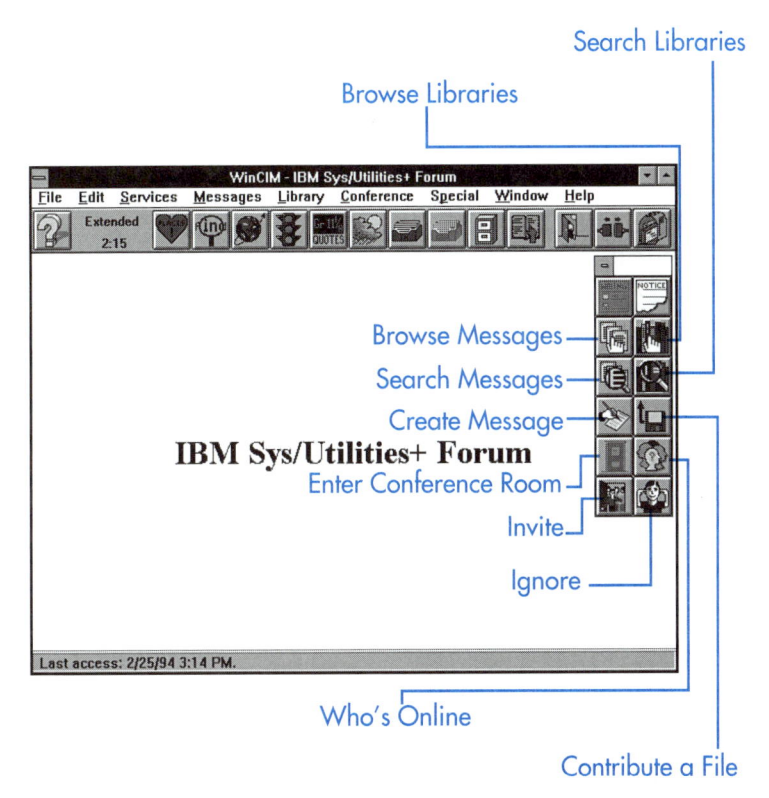

Figure 20.1   The Forum desktop and Toolbox.

CompuServe designed the icons to take you in and out of forum areas and complete forum activities. (Notice that the menu bar is also different for forums.) The most frequently used Toolbox icons are:

- **Browse Messages**   Displays message Sections to browse.

- **Search Messages** For finding information on specific subjects.
- **Browse Libraries** Displays the Library Sections to browse.
- **Search Libraries** For finding a specific file or program.

Searching a Forum for a Program

Let's try an example to get comfortable with searching a forum. You will use the Search Library icon to find a utility file called PKZIP. This program and the related program PKUNZIP, condense and expand files so you can quickly transfer them over CompuServe (see Lesson 15 and Appendix D). As you use forums and download files, you will often need PKZIP.

To download PKZIP from CompuServe follow these steps (Note: following these steps will cost about $1—but it's money well spent.):

1. Click the Go icon. The Go dialog box appears.

2. Type IBMCOM (for the IBM Communications Forum).

3. Press Enter. You connect to CompuServe (if you weren't already) and enter the IBM Communications Forum. A dialog box asks if you want to join.

4. Click Join (it costs nothing extra). You enter the forum, and the desktop and Toolbar (and possibly an introductory screen) appear.

5. (Optional) Click OK if you get a window labeled **News Flash**. In some cases, you have to wait while a forum logo automatically downloads.

6. Click the Search Libraries icon. The Search for Files dialog box appears.

Using Forums **125**

7. Enter **PK204G.EXE** in the File Name text box.

8. Click Search or press Enter. WinCIM finds the file and displays it in the Library Search box.

9. Double-click the highlighted entry or click Description for more information about the program (see Figure 20.2).

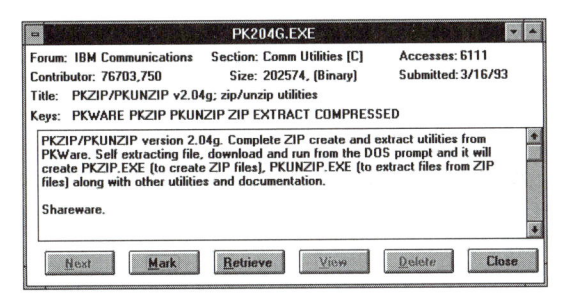

```
                        PK204G.EXE
Forum: IBM Communications   Section: Comm Utilities [C]   Accesses: 6111
Contributor: 76703,750       Size: 202574, (Binary)        Submitted: 3/16/93
Title:   PKZIP/PKUNZIP v2.04g; zip/unzip utilities
Keys:    PKWARE PKZIP PKUNZIP ZIP EXTRACT COMPRESSED

PKZIP/PKUNZIP version 2.04g. Complete ZIP create and extract utilities from
PKWare. Self extracting file, download and run from the DOS prompt and it will
create PKZIP.EXE (to create ZIP files), PKUNZIP.EXE (to extract files from ZIP
files) along with other utilities and documentation.

Shareware.

    Next     Mark    Retrieve    View    Delete    Close
```

Figure 20.2 The Search for Files dialog box finds files or programs in the library.

Search Options Often, you don't know the exact name of the program or file you are looking for. Then you can use the Keyword option and type in a more general description of the file. In this case, you could type **PKZIP** to find several versions of the program.

Go Forums All of CompuServe's forums have their own quick reference words. When you type one of these quick reference words after clicking on the Go icon, you proceed to that forum's opening menu. You can find quick reference words for all the Forums by typing **Quick** after clicking on the Go icon. Then select option 2: List ALL Indexed Topics.

Downloading a Forum File

You have now located the file you need. To download it to your computer, follow these steps:

1. Click Retrieve in the file description box labeled **PK204G.EXE**. The Save As dialog box appears.

2. Click OK. A bar graph appears as the file downloads (see Figure 20.3). It will take about three minutes to retrieve the file at 9600 baud rate.

3. Click the Disconnect icon in the Ribbon to leave CompuServe when the bar graph disappears. (A message along the bottom of the screen will read **C:\CSERVE\DOWNLOAD\PK204G.EXE transferred successfully**.)

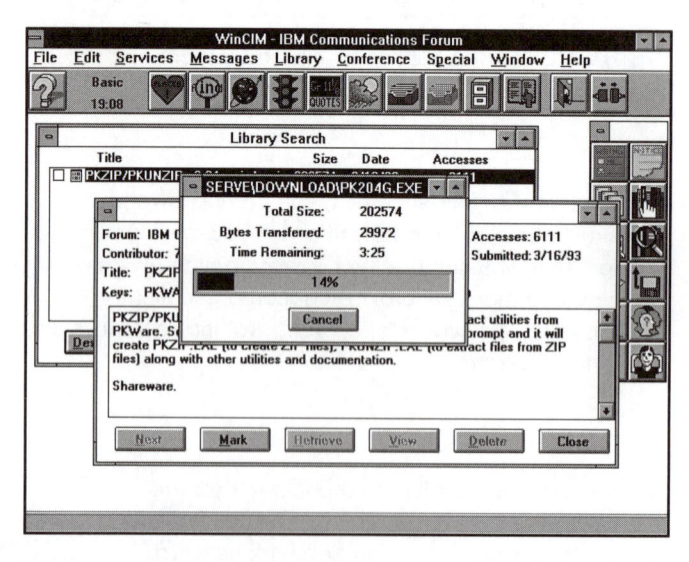

Figure 20.3 This bar graph appears during downloads.

All forum files—text files, programs and graphics—are downloaded in this way. Once in your system, you may want to move the file to another subdirectory (see Lesson 16). To use PKZIP and PKUNZIP see Appendix D.

In this lesson, you learned how to search for a program in a Forum and download it to your computer system. In the next lesson, you will learn how to post a message on a CompuServe forum.

Lesson 21

Joining Forums and Posting Messages

In this lesson, you'll learn how to reply to a forum message while online and how to create a forum message offline.

Finding Your Forum

Before you can post a forum message, you must join a forum. Before you join a forum, you have to find one that interests you. With over 600 forums on CompuServe to choose from, and more being added all the time, narrowing the field is difficult.

One way to locate your forum is to use the Find icon (see Lesson 4). After you click the Find icon, a dialog box appears. You can just enter the name of your interest. If you want to browse all forums, type FORUM.

Browsing a Forum

Once inside a forum, you can browse the Message Sections and messages to see if they are of interest to you (see Figure 21.1). Read some of the threads to get an idea of the tone of the messages that people exchange.

> **Thread** A series of forum messages on a certain subject that all have the same title. The thread consists of messages by many different forum members.

Plain English

Joining Forums and Posting Messages — 129

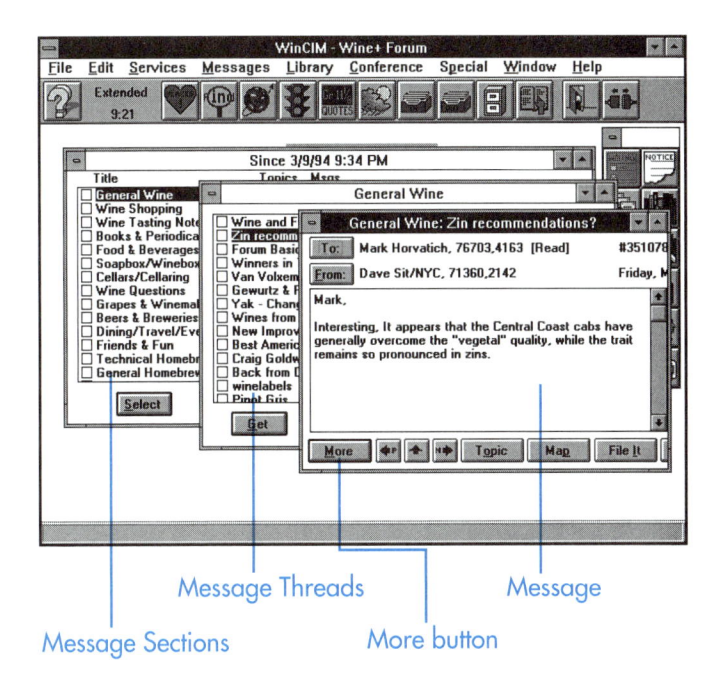

Figure 21.1 Message Sections, message subjects, and a sample message.

For an example of how to browse forum messages, try looking at the Bacchus Wine Forum. (If you would rather explore a different forum, get online, go to the Services window, and click the Forum icon. Choose a forum that looks interesting, and then jump to Step 4.)

To browse messages in the Bacchus Wine Forum, follow these steps:

1. Click the Home/Leisure icon in the Services group window. You are connected to CompuServe, and the Home/Leisure menu opens.

2. Double-click Food/Wine. The Food/Wine menu opens.

3. Double-click the Bacchus Wine Forum +. You enter the forum.

4. (Optional) Click the Join button if this is your first visit to the forum.

5. (Optional) Click OK if another screen displays forum notices.

6. Click the Browse Messages icon. A window opens listing the Message Sections.

7. Choose a subject of interest and double-click on it. A listing of all message topics appears.

8. Find a subject that looks interesting and double-click on it. The first in a series of messages appears.

9. Click the More button (see Figure 21.1) to see the rest of the message, if it's more than one screen, or to open the next message in the thread.

10. Disconnect and close the Forum Toolbox by clicking on the Disconnect icon. If you want to stay online and reply to one of the messages you see, refer to the next section.

Replying to a Forum Message

When reading a forum thread, you will eventually get the urge to put in your two cents. WinCIM makes this fast and easy to do. However, don't ponder over your choice of words as you type your reply—it's costing you money to remain in this extended service.

With the message you want to answer on the screen, follow these steps to reply to it:

1. Click the Reply button. The Reply to Forum Message box opens.

2. Enter your reply. Notice that the Send button becomes active when you enter text.

3. Click the Send button. The message becomes part of the thread under the Library section you are in.

4. Disconnect and close the Forum Toolbox by clicking on the Disconnect icon.

Creating a Forum Message

There will be times when you want to start a new thread or post a question in a forum message section. To lower your expense, it's best to create such a message offline, put it in your Out-Basket, and then send it when you have finished it.

These are the steps required to create a forum message:

1. Click on the Mail command on the menu bar.

2. Click on Create Forum Message. The Create Forum Message dialog opens (see Figure 21.2).

3. Click the down arrow to the right of the Forum button. This pulls down a list of the forums you belong to.

Lesson 21

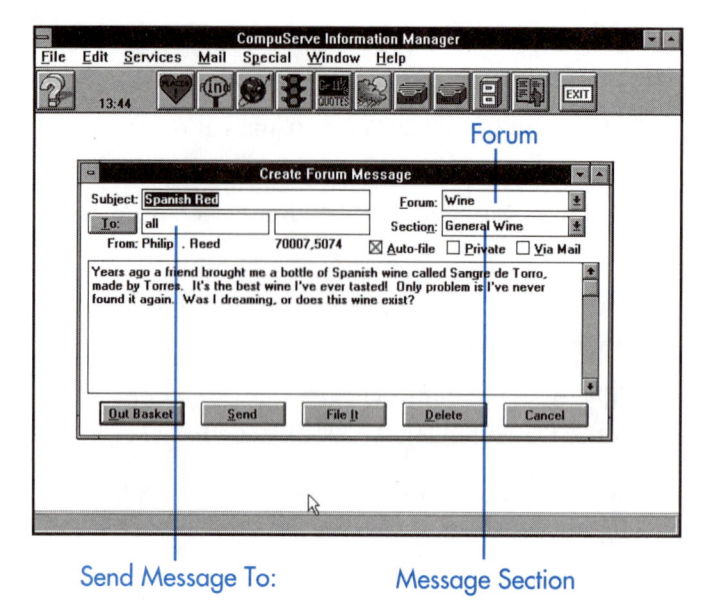

Figure 21.2 The Create Forum Message dialog box.

4. Select the forum your message is for and click on it. The box closes.

5. Click the down arrow button to the right of the Section button. This pulls down a list of the Message Sections.

6. Select the Message Section your message is for and click on it. The box closes.

7. Move your cursor to the Subject box and give the message a title.

8. Move your cursor into the TO: box, and type the name of the recipient. (If your message is for everyone in the forum, type **All**. If you have a question on how the forum works, type **Sysop**.)

9. Type your message.

10. Click the Out-Basket button. The Message dialog box closes.

With your forum message in your Out-Basket, you can send it as you would an e-mail message (see Lesson 12).

> **Cut Forum Costs** The Disconnect When Done option of the Send/Receive All Mail command is particularly valuable when using CompuServe forums. You stay connected to a forum just long enough to download the message.

In this lesson, you learned how to browse forum message sections, reply to a message online, and create your own message offline. In the next lesson, you will learn how to search for good financial investments online.

Lesson 22

Financial Services

In this lesson, you will learn about some of CompuServe's financial services and how to get online stock quotes.

Managing Your Money

CompuServe provides many valuable services to help you manage both your personal and business finances. Here are just a few of the many financial activities you can perform on CompuServe:

- Calculate your net worth.
- Generate a loan amortization schedule.
- Find and communicate with brokers.
- Communicate with other investors in financial forums.
- Search for financial information about a specific company or business.

Perhaps the most widely used feature offered by CompuServe is the ability to get quotes for U.S. stocks, options, indexes, exchange rates, and mutual funds. You can also chart the history of a stock and build a portfolio of your stocks' performance.

Checking Your Stocks

CompuServe delays the quotes 15 minutes (as required by the exchange), and you can retrieve up to 20 quotes in a single session. The first time you use the quotes feature you have to supply information about the stocks you hold. CompuServe stores this information and subsequently you can quickly get a picture of your stocks' performance.

Inputting Your Stocks

To get a quote for a stock, you first have to tell WinCIM what stocks you hold. To add your stocks' ticker symbols, follow these steps:

1. Click the Quotes icon on the Ribbon. A Quotes dialog box opens (see Figure 22.1).

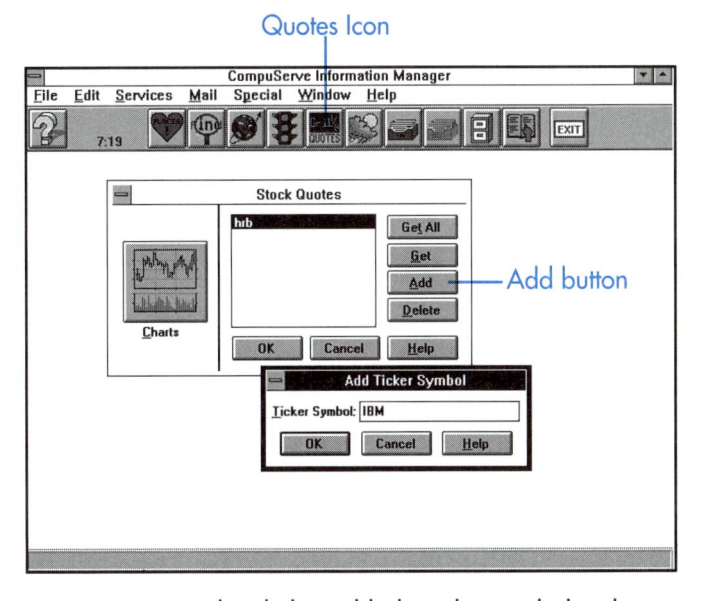

Figure 22.1 This dialog adds the ticker symbol to the Stock Quotes box.

2. Click the Add button. An Add Ticker Symbol box opens (see Figure 22.1). If you don't know the ticker symbol for your stock, see the next section.

3. Type the ticker symbol in the Add Ticker Symbol box.

4. Click OK. CompuServe adds your stock's ticker symbol to the Quotes dialog box.

5. (Optional) Repeat steps 2–4 for the other stocks you hold.

Looking Up a Ticker Symbol

CompuServe provides a powerful tool for finding a stock's ticker symbol (the sequence of letters that represents a stock). To find a stock's ticker symbol, follow these steps:

1. Click the Charts button in the Quotes dialog box. You connect to CompuServe (if you weren't already) and leave basic services. A Price Volume Graph dialog box opens.

2. Click the Lookup button. A Security Search dialog box opens (see Figure 22.2). Type in the company name.

3. Click the All button unless you know how the stock is categorized.

4. Click the Search button. A dialog box appears listing all the stocks that match your search criteria (see Figure 22.3).

Financial Services   **137**

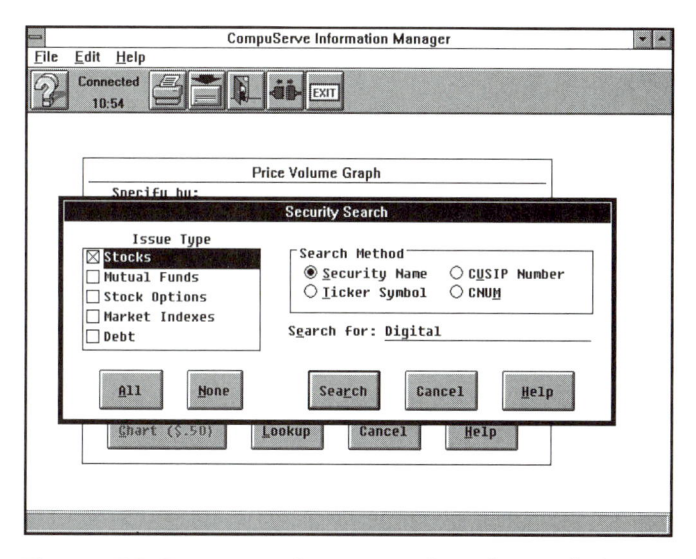

Figure 22.2 You can locate a stock's ticker symbol using this box.

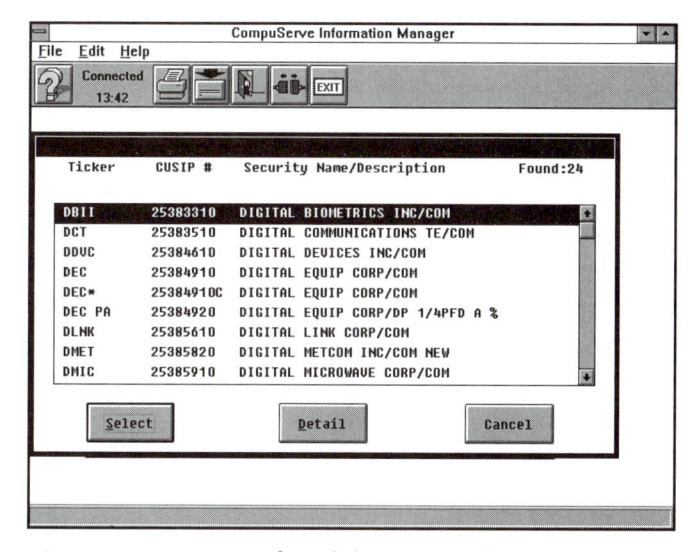

Figure 22.3 Issues found during a stock search.

5. Highlight the issue you want.

6. Click the Select button. You return to the Price Volume Graph dialog box. The ticker symbol automatically inserts here.

> **GO LOOKUP** To quickly search a stock's ticker symbol, click the GO icon and type **LOOKUP**.

Charting a Stock's Performance

Now that you've found the ticker symbol, you can see how your stock has performed. To see a chart of your stock's history, follow these steps (Note: this will cost $.50):

1. Choose the time period by clicking in the circle under Periodicity.

2. Click the Chart ($.50) button. A chart appears in a dialog box with your stock's ticker symbol (see Figure 22.4).

3. (Optional) Save the chart by double-clicking on the Control-menu box in the left corner of the graphic screen. A dialog box appears.

4. (Optional) Click Yes if you want to save the graph. The Save As dialog box appears telling you where the chart will be saved and the file name.

5. (Optional) Click OK. The Save As dialog box and the Graphics dialog box close.

6. Click the Cancel button in the Price Volume Graph dialog box. You leave extended services and return to the WinCIM desktop.

Financial Services 139

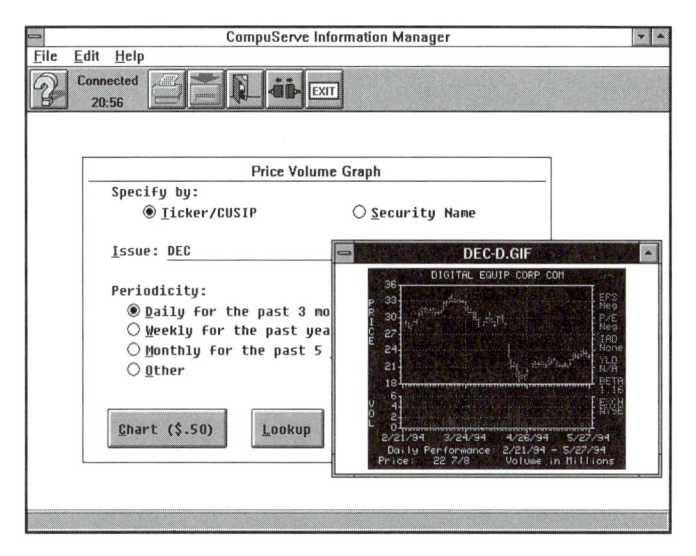

Figure 22.4 CompuServe can chart a stock's recent performance.

Getting a Stock Quote

Now that you know your stock's ticker symbol, you can get the latest quote on its market value. To get a stock quote, follow these steps:

1. Click the Quotes icon. The Stock Quotes dialog box opens.

2. (Optional) Include or remove stocks using the Add and Delete buttons.

3. Click on Get All. A Quotes Information dialog box appears listing the most recent market figures (see Figure 22.5).

Lesson 22

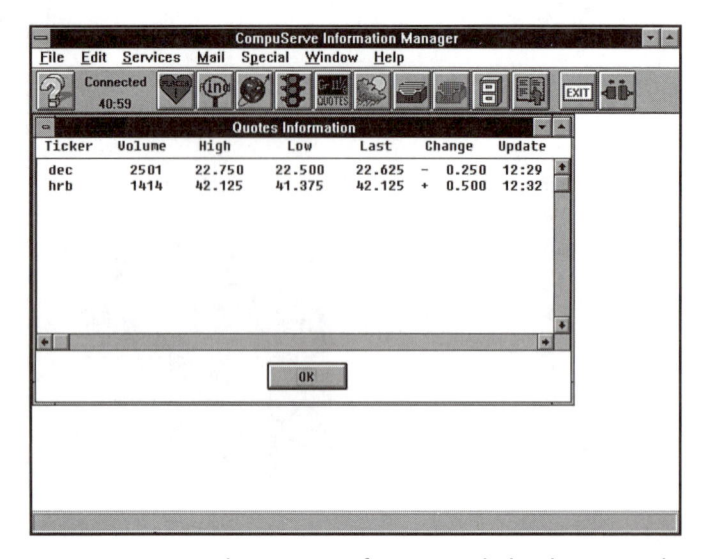

[screenshot of CompuServe Information Manager Quotes Information dialog box showing:]

```
Ticker  Volume  High    Low     Last    Change    Update
dec     2501    22.750  22.500  22.625  - 0.250   12:29
hrb     1414    42.125  41.375  42.125  + 0.500   12:32
```

Figure 22.5 The Quotes Information dialog box provides the market's latest figures.

4. Click OK to return the WinCIM desktop.

5. Click Disconnect to disconnect from CompuServe.

> **Stock Portfolio** CompuServe offers a way to easily record your stock purchases and analyze their market performance. Click Services on the menu bar, and then select Portfolio to get the Stock Portfolio dialog box. After filling in the blanks under Add Portfolio Entry, you can generate a report that shows your portfolio's total gain or loss.

Personal and Business Financial Services

While CompuServe's designed the financial services for the private investor, they are powerful enough for financial experts to use. If your business depends on the stock market, take some time to fully investigate all the financial services provided by CompuServe.

In this lesson, you learned how to get the latest quotes for your stocks and how to chart a stock's performance. In the next lesson, you'll learn how to customize WinCIM.

Lesson 23

Customizing WinCIM

In this lesson, you will learn how to change the way WinCIM looks and works to suit your personal preferences.

Creating Your Own Work Environment

By now, you are familiar with the way WinCIM performs. Along with your knowledge, you have probably developed some likes and dislikes about how this program operates. Fortunately, you can change many of the things about WinCIM to suit your own personal taste. Now it's time to act on your preferences—to tailor WinCIM to exactly the way you like it.

The following steps will take you to the different areas of the program where WinCIM can be modified. However, it's up to you to decide how you want WinCIM changed. In some cases, you may not know what you want to change yet. That's okay. You can always revisit these areas after you get more experience working with WinCIM.

Visiting Session Settings

To view the settings that control your use of CompuServe, follow these steps:

1. With WinCIM loaded, click Special on the menu bar. The Special pull-down menu appears.

2. Click Session Settings. The Setup Session Settings dialog box appears (see Figure 23.1).

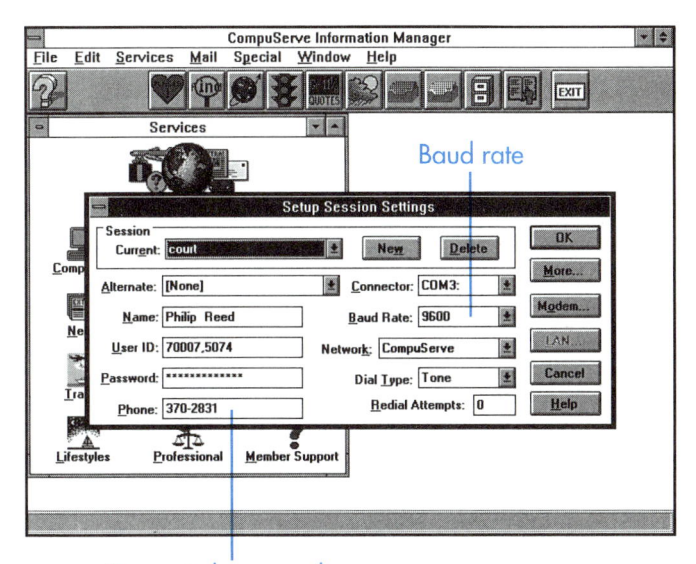

Customizing WinCIM 143

[Screenshot of CompuServe Information Manager showing Setup Session Settings dialog box, with "Baud rate" label pointing to the Baud Rate field (9600) and "Connect phone number" label pointing to the Phone field (370-2831).]

Figure 23.1 If you change the baud rate, you will need a new connect phone number.

The settings should look familiar because you chose them when you went through the sign-up process. You won't be changing anything now. However, this dialog box may be necessary to you in the future for a number of reasons, including:

- If you get a faster modem and need to change the baud rate at which you connect to CompuServe.
- If you want to change your password.
- If you want to change the access number you use to connect to CompuServe.

Increasing Baud Rate Make sure that you set the baud rate specified in the Setup Session Settings dialog box for the highest rate your modem is capable of. If necessary, change the setting in the Baud Rate box. If you do this, you will also have to change your access in the phone box. You can get a new access number by logging onto CompuServe, clicking the Go icon, and typing in **PHONES**.

Changing Preferences

On the same menu, a different command enables you to change the way you interact with WinCIM. Several recommendations appear in this section. You may later reverse these changes or make additional modifications based on your needs and experiences.

To make changes under Preferences:

1. Close the Setup Session Settings dialog box by clicking the Cancel box.

2. Click Special on the menu bar. The Special menu appears.

3. Click Preferences on the Special menu. A sub-menu appears.

4. Click General on the Preferences sub-menu. The General Preferences dialog box opens (see Figure 23.2). (Note: this option is not available in WinCIM before version 1.5.)

5. Click About Box so that no **X** appears in it.

6. (Optional) Click the Browse box so no X appears in it. Doing this tells WinCIM not to open the Services window when you load the program. After you get the hang of using the GO icon, you won't really need the Services window. In addition, you can use shortcut keys to access menus when the Services window is closed, and the screen is less cluttered. If, at some point, you need the Services window open, click the Browse icon.

Customizing WinCIM   **145**

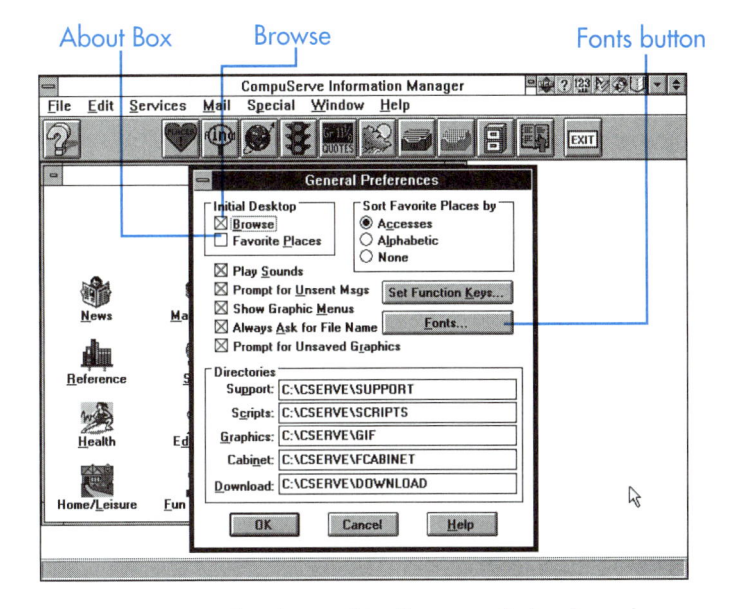

Figure 23.2 The General Preferences dialog box changes the way WinCIM looks and works.

7. Notice the Fonts button. If, as you use CompuServe more, you decide you want to change the fonts (the type used in CompuServe messages and dialog boxes), click this button. You can choose the font that suits your taste or is easier to read. CompuServe can use the fonts used in Windows applications.

8. Click the OK button to close the General Preferences dialog box and save your change or changes.

> **Unsaved Changes** Throughout WinCIM, you will find boxes, such as the General Preferences dialog box. When making changes in these dialog boxes, click OK. If you click the Cancel button, WinCIM *does not* save your changes.

In this final lesson, you learned how to use the Setup Session Settings and General Preferences dialog boxes to modify the look and operation of WinCIM.

Appendix A

Windows Basics

Tell Me About Windows

Microsoft Windows is a graphical interface program that makes your computer easier to use by enabling you to select menu items and pictures rather than type commands. Before you can take advantage of it, however, you must learn some Windows basics.

Starting Microsoft Windows

To start Windows, do the following:

1. At the DOS prompt, type **win**.

2. Press Enter.

The Windows title screen appears for a few moments, and then you see a screen like the one in Figure A.1.

> **What If It Didn't Work?** You may have to change to the Windows directory before starting Windows; to do so, type **CD\WINDOWS** and press Enter.

Appendix A

Figure A.1: Parts of a Windows screen, with labels: Control - menu box, Title bar, Minimize button, Menu bar, Mouse pointer, Program group icons, Program-items icons, Scroll bar, Maximize buttton

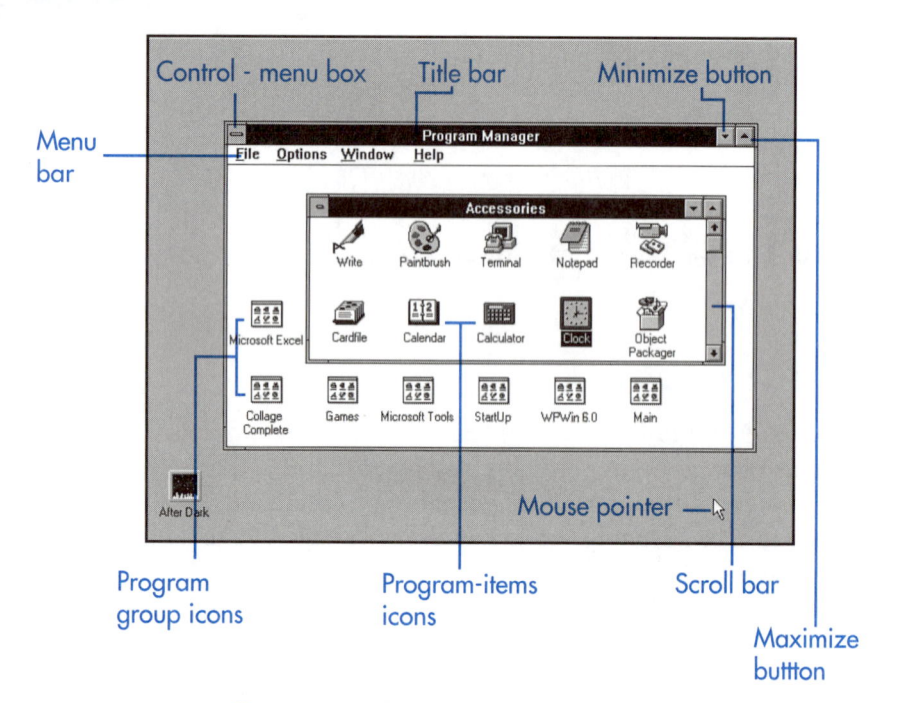

Parts of a Windows Screen

As shown in Figure A.1, the Windows screen contains several unique elements that you won't see in DOS. Here's a brief summary:

- *Title bar*—Shows the name of the window or program.

- *Program group windows*—Contain program icons that allow you to run programs.

- *Icons*—Graphic representations of programs. To run a program, you select its icon.

- *Minimize and Maximize buttons*—Alter a window's size. The Minimize button shrinks the window to the size of an icon. The Maximize button expands the window to fill the screen. When maximized, a window contains a double-arrow *Restore* button, which returns the window to its original size.

- *Control-menu box*—When selected, pulls down a menu that offers size and location controls for the window.

- *Pull-down menu bar*—Contains a list of the pull-down menus available in the program.

- *Mouse Pointer*—If you are using a mouse, the mouse pointer (usually an arrow) appears on-screen. You can control it by moving the mouse (discussed later in this appendix).

- *Scroll bars*—If a window contains more information than can be displayed in the window, a scroll bar appears. *Scroll arrows* on each end of the scroll bar allow you to scroll slowly. The *scroll box* allows you to scroll more quickly.

Using a Mouse

To work most efficiently in Windows, you should use a mouse. You can press mouse buttons and move the mouse in various ways to change the way it acts:

Point means to move the mouse pointer onto the specified item by moving the mouse. The tip of the mouse pointer must be touching the item.

Click on an item means to move the pointer onto the specified item and press the mouse button once. Unless specified otherwise, use the left mouse button.

Double-click on an item means to move the pointer onto the specified item and press and release the mouse button twice quickly.

Drag means to move the mouse pointer onto the specified item, hold down the mouse button, and move the mouse while holding down the button.

Appendix A

You can use the mouse to perform common Windows activities, including running applications and moving and resizing windows.

Starting a Program

To start a program, simply double-click on its icon (or Tab to it and press Enter). If its icon is in a program group window that's not open at the moment, open the window first. Follow these steps:

1. If necessary, open the program group window that contains the program you want to run. To open a program group window, click on its icon.

2. Double-click on the icon for the program you want to run.

Using Menus

The pull-down menu bar (see Figure A.2) contains various menus from which you can select commands. Each Windows program that you run has a set of pull-down menus; Windows itself has a set, too.

To open a menu, click on its name on the menu bar. Once a menu is open, you can select a command from it by clicking on the desired command.

> **What Are Accelerator keys?** Notice that in Figure A.2, key names follow some commands, such as **Enter** (for the **Open** command) or **F8** (for the **Copy** command). These are *accelerator keys*. You can use these keys to perform these commands without even opening the menu.

Windows Basics   **151**

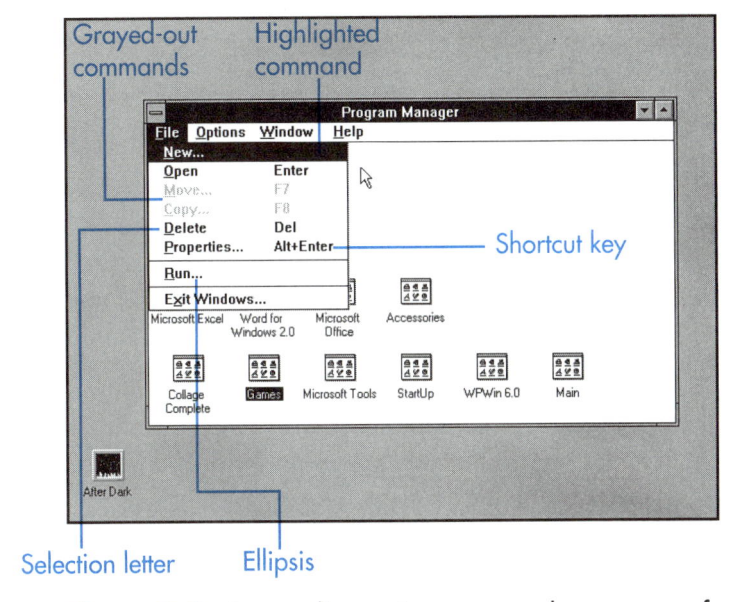

Figure A.2 A menu lists various commands you can perform.

Usually, when you select a command, Windows performs the command immediately. However:

- If the command name is gray (rather than black), the command is unavailable at the moment, and you cannot choose it.

- If an arrow follows the command name, selecting the command will cause another menu to appear, from which you select another command.

- If an ellipsis (three dots) follows the command name, selecting the command will cause a dialog box to appear. You'll learn about dialog boxes in the next section.

Navigating Dialog Boxes

A dialog box is Windows' way of requesting additional information. For example, if you choose Print from Write's menu, you'll see the dialog box shown in Figure A.3.

Appendix A

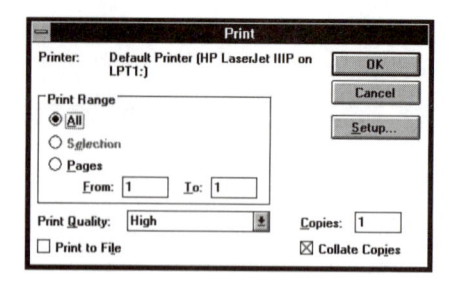

[A screenshot of a Print dialog box showing Printer, Print Range (All, Selection, Pages From/To), Print Quality, Copies, Print to File, Collate Copies, and OK/Cancel/Setup buttons.]

Figure A.3 A typical dialog box.

Each dialog box contains one or more of the following elements:

- *List boxes* display available choices. To activate a list, click inside the list box. If the entire list is not visible, use the scroll bar to view the items in the list. To select an item from the list, click on it.

- *Drop-down lists* are similar to list boxes, but only one item in the list appears. To see the rest of the items, click on the down arrow to the right of the list box. To select an item from the list, click on it.

- *Text boxes* allow you to type an entry. To activate a text box, click inside it. To edit an existing entry, use the arrow keys to move the cursor; the Del or Backspace keys to delete existing characters; and then type your correction.

- *Check boxes* allow you to select one or more items in a group of options. For example, if you are styling text, you may select Bold and Italic to have the text appear in both bold type and italic type. Click on a check box to activate it.

- *Option buttons* are like check boxes, but you can select only one option button in a group. Selecting one button unselects any option that you previously selected. Click on an option button to activate it.

- *Command buttons* execute (or cancel) the command once you have made your selections in the dialog box. To press a command button, click on it.

Switching Between Windows

Many times, you will have more than one window open at once. Some open windows may be program group windows, while others may be actual programs that are running. To switch among them, you can:

- Pull down the Window menu, and choose the window you want to view; or
- If a portion of the desired window is visible, click on it.

Controlling a Window

As you saw earlier in this appendix, you can minimize, maximize, and restore windows on your screen. However, you can also move them and change their size.

- To move a window, drag its title bar to a different location. (Remember, "drag" means to hold down the left mouse button while you move the mouse.)
- To resize a window, position the mouse pointer on the border of the window until you see a double-headed arrow; then drag the window border to the desired size.

Appendix B

Working with Modems

Working with modems is perhaps the most difficult and frustrating part of going on-line. In most cases, you will successfully connect to CompuServe and will never again have to think about your modem. However, the time may come when you upgrade to a new modem, or add an accessory to your computer system and suddenly find you can't reconnect.

If you like a challenge and are technically oriented, you will find many like-minded people and lots of great information on any one of the CompuServe forums, such as the IBM Communications Forum.

If you know little about modems, and aren't interested in doing anything more than making the thing work, there are still several steps you can take to solve your problem and a few tips that will avoid further problems.

Failure to Connect with CompuServe

The most common problem beginners face when trying to connect with CompuServe is to set their comunications port (COM port) correctly. Obviously, this stems from not knowing the setting on their COM port. It seems this should be a simple problem to fix since there are only four possible settings: COM port 1, 2, 3, or 4. However, there are several factors that can complicate the situation.

Locating the COM Port

First, keep in mind that the COM port has nothing to do with where, physically, you place the modem. Looking at the back of the computer and counting the slots in your motherboard won't give you the answer. Jumper switches, or dip switches, on the modem itself control the COM port setting. Your goal is to find out the modem setting, and then change the setting in your computer to match that.

Read the documentation that came with the modem to learn how the factory set the COM port. If you can clearly determine this, set your COM port for the same location within CompuServe.

If, after setting your modem to the factory setting, you still can't connect with CompuServe, then you may have a conflict with your mouse. The mouse also connects to one of the COM ports—usually 1. To find out your mouse setting, try running a Microsoft diagnostic program that comes with Windows. Exit Windows and type **C:\WINDOWS\MSD** at the DOS prompt. All the mouse settings appear under Mouse.

Get back into Windows and load WinCIM. Under Session Settings, change the modem COM port to 3 or 4 if the mouse setting is 1 or 2.

Setting Modem Jumper and Dip Switches

Perhaps you have determined that your mouse setting is COM port 2 and the factory setting for your modem is also 2. Clearly, you have a conflict. This means you will have to change the modem jumper switches or dip switches.

Dip switches are usually small toggle switches that are set **on** or **off**; **up** or **down**. In your modem instructions, you will find a table that tells you how to set the dip switches for each of the COM ports. With your computer turned off and unplugged, use the tip of a pen to carefully set these dip switches so your modem does not conflict with your mouse.

Jumper switches are small rectangular plastic objects that electronically connect two pins on the modem board. You can pull these off and place them in different positions. Again, with your computer turned off and unplugged, carefully rearrange the jumper switches (according to the settings in your modem documentation) so your modem does not conflict with your mouse.

This setup may require trial and error. Be patient. In between tests, turn the computer completely off since the changes may not take effect unless you shut the power down.

Other Modem Related Problems

Once you are up and running, you may still have occasional problems that you can trace back to your modem. The most common problem is becoming disconnected from CompuServe. If you are in the middle of downloading a file, you will have to start again from the beginning. This wastes time and money.

Call Waiting

The most common cause of disconnection is call waiting. If you connect with CompuServe on a phone line that has call waiting, an incoming call will often ring through. WinCIM may lock up as a result. It's also possible that the interruption from call waiting will disconnect you from CompuServe but not ring through. You may wonder what happened as WinCIM fails to respond any longer.

Some telephone companies offer an added feature that turns off call waiting. This is worth it if you frequently download or upload large files.

To avoid call waiting interruptions you can also connect with CompuServe at hours when considerate people won't be telephoning you. If you are on the alternate plan, this makes good sense for another reason: connect time charges are lower.

Other Disconnect Causes

In some cases, *line noise* can cause you to disconnect from CompuServe. Try redialing. You will get a different—and possibly better—connection. If there is an electrical storm in your area, this can cause real problems with your connection—not to mention damage to your computer. Turn off your system and unplug it until the storm has passed.

If disconnection problems are frequent, it could be the condition of the line leading into your house. Call your phone company to see if they can test the line, install a filter, or recondition your line.

Changing Baud Rates

If you get a new modem that is capable of faster comunications speeds, you will have to change your baud rate setting. You will also have to change the connect phone number. The telephone number setting you use is for only one baud rate.

To find a new number, at a higher baud rate, click the GO icon, and type in **Phones**. You can search for a new number based on your area code.

Appendix

The Cost of Services

Before you use any service on CompuServe you should know what it will cost you. You can always find the most recent costs by clicking the GO icon and typing RATES. You can usually find pricing information in the introductory window of any extended services.

For quick reference, here is a brief review of how CompuServe charges you.

Two Payment Plans

There are two basic ways to pay for CompuServe: the Standard Pricing Plan (also called Flat-rate), and the Alternative Pricing Plan (also called Pay-as-you-go). Here are the main features of each plan.

Standard Pricing Plan

Under this plan, you pay $8.95 per month (the first month you join is free) and receive unlimited connect-time for the basic services. This includes a $9.00 allowance for e-mail postage. CompuServe charges you for extended or premium services at "hourly connect rates" based on the baud rate of your modem (see chart below). CompuServe bills you in one-minute increments with a minimum of one minute per session.

The Cost of Services

Standard Pricing Plan:

300 baud .... $ 4.80/hour

1200, 2400 baud .... $ 4.80/hour

9600, 14400 baud .... $ 9.60/hour

Some services carry additional premium surcharges. For example, databases often charge a connect time fee, plus $1.50 or more for downloading an article.

Alternative Pricing Plan

If you don't anticipate being online very long (maybe you will just be using the e-mail features of CompuServe) you may want to try the Alternative Pricing Plan.

Alternative Pricing Plan:

300 baud .... $ 6.30/hour

1200, 2400 baud. $12.80/hour

9600, 14400 baud. $22.80/hour

In addition to these connect time rates, some services may also carry a premium surcharge.

CompuServe Product Categories

As you browse CompuServe services and consider using them, refer to this chart of pricing codes to let you know roughly how much it will cost:

Type of Service	Cost	Symbol
Basic	Flat monthly fee	None
Extended	Hourly	+
Premium	Hourly & surcharge	$
Executive	Hourly/surcharge/membership	$E

Appendix

File Compression

In Lesson 20, you downloaded a file compression program from the IBM COMunications Forum. That program is PK204G.EXE and it is a version of the popular PK shareware programs.

PKZIP compresses files while PKUNZIP restores them to their normal size so your computer can read and use them. Additionally, PKZIP takes a number of files and compresses them into one file. This simplifies the process of sending files through CompuServe and also speeds things up considerably.

PKZIP can actually do many related chores. You can find complete instructions in the MANUAL.DOC file that you will see momentarily. Here are the instructions for setting up this program and zipping and unzipping files.

Setting Up PK204g.EXE

Follow these steps to setup up PKZIP for use:

1. Double click File Manager in Windows. File manager opens.

2. Click File on the menu bar.

3. Click the Create Directory command. A Create Directory dialog box opens.

4. Type ZIP in the Create Directory dialog box (or whatever you want to name the directory). The directory is created and the box closes.

File Compression

5. Click the CSERVE directory in the left box. The CSERVE subdirectories open in the right-hand section of the screen.

6. Click the DOWNLOAD subdirectory. The files in this subdirectory are listed in the right-hand section of the screen.

7. Highlight the PK204G.EXE file.

8. Click on File on the menu bar.

9. Click the Move command. A Move dialog box appears.

10. Type c:\ZIP*.* in the **TO:** blank in the dialog box.

11. Click OK. The file PK204G.EXE moves to the directory ZIP.

Using PKZIP

To use PKZIP and PKUNZIP, you must first decompress the file you downloaded. PK204G.EXE is a *self-extracting* file. This means it will expand into a number of individual, compressed files. Follow these steps to extract these files:

1. Exit Windows.

2. Type C:\ZIP.

3. Press Enter.

4. Type PK204G.EXE. Sixteen files are automatically created.

Among the files that now exist is MANUAL.DOC, which contains complete instructions for using PKZIP and PKUNZIP. There are many special features to PK software. However, the two most commonly used are PKZIP and PKUNZIP.

Zipping a File

To compress, or "zip" a single file, use this format:

C:\ZIP\PKZIP C:\[*name of zip file you will create*] C:\[*name of file to zip*]

In other words, you tell the computer where to find the PKZIP program, tell the PKZIP program what file you want to create, and then tell it which file to compress.

For example, if you had a file named PRACTICE in the C:\TEMP directory, this is how you would zip it:

C:\ZIP\PKZIP C:\TEMP\PRACTICE.ZIP C:\TEMP\PRACTICE

Zipping Multiple Files

By adding **-a** to the above command string, you can take multiple files and compress them into a single zip file. For example, if you had a series of files for a book, all in the C:\TEMP directory, which you named CHAP1.DOC, CHAP2.DOC, CHAP3.DOC, and you wanted to send them all to your editor, this is how you would make one compressed file:

C:\ZIP\PKZIP -a C:\TEMP\CHAP.ZIP C:\TEMP*.DOC

Unzipping Files

The process for unzipping multiple files is the same as for unzipping a single file. You merely designate where PKUNZIP is, and which file you want unzipped. If you wanted the file C:\TEMP\PRACTICE.ZIP unzipped, this is how you would do it:

C:\ZIP\PKUNZIP C:\TEMP\PRACTICE.ZIP

File Compression

Using this format, all the compressed files in PRACTICE.ZIP would expand and be placed in your C:\TEMP directory. If you wanted those files expanded and placed somewhere else, write the format this way:

C:\ZIP\PKUNZIP C:\TEMP\PRACTICE.ZIP C:\TEMP\PRACTICE

A word of caution: when you decompress a zipped file, you never really know what you are getting. It could expand into many smaller files that are all meant to be grouped in the same directory. If you expand the files into the wrong directory, and then attempt to move them, you might get them mixed up with files from other software applications. Therefore, it's best to move the zipped file into the desired directory before unzipping it.

Index

A-B

Academic American Encyclopedia, 55-57
account information, 9-11
Add to Address Book dialog box, 69
Address Book, 68-69
    adding addresses, 69-70
    copying addresses, 71-72
    managing, 72-74
    searching Member Directory, 70-71
    writing e-mail messages, 77
Air/Hotel/Car, 114-117
alternative pricing plan, 5, 159
Associated Press Online, 47-50
automating Mail, 87-88

Bacchus Wine Forum, 129
baud rates, 5
    changing, 157
    customizing, 143
binary files, 93
Browse icon, 55
browsing forums, 128-130

C

call waiting, 156-157
charting stock performance, 138-139
Close All command (Windows menu), 50
closing windows, 50
commands, *see* individual command names
communications ports, 9, 155
compressing files, 160-163
CompuServe, 1-2
    connecting to, 16-17
    disconnecting from, 17-18
    signing up, 6-9
CompuServe Information Manager for Windows, *see* WinCIM
CompuServe Weather Reports dialog box, 50
connecting to CompuServe, 16-17
context-sensitive help (WinCIM), 30-32
copying
    addresses to Address Book, 71-72
    e-mail, 87
    text (Notepad documents), 44
Create Forum Message command (Mail menu), 131
Create Mail command (Mail menu), 77
customer service, 35
customizing WinCIM
    Preferences command (Special menu), 144-146
    Session Settings command (Special menu), 142
cutting text (Notepad documents), 44

Index

D

decompressing files, 162-163
departments (shopping), 110-112
desktop (WinCIM), 13-15
dialog boxes, *see* individual dialog box names
dip switches, 155-156
disconnect problems, 157
disconnecting from CompuServe, 17-18
downloading files, 27, 36-38
    e-mail, 84-85
    forums, 126-127
    from Mail, 96-97
    help information, 34-35
    Magazine Database Plus (CIM), 66
    moving files, 98-100

E

e-mail, *see* Mail
EAASY SABRE (CIM), 114-117
    fares, 117-118
    itineraries, 119-120
Edit menu commands (Notepad)
    Undo, 44-45
    Word Wrap, 43
editing Notepad documents, 43-44
Electronic Mall, 107
    departments, 110-112
    entering, 108-109
    QuickSearch, 112-113
encyclopedia, 55-57
Executive Services, 27
exiting
    Leave icon, 59
    WinCIM, 17-18
exporting files, 40
external modems, 1

F

fares (travel), 117-118
Favorite Places icon, 23-24
File It button, 86-87
File Manager
    moving files, 98-100
    PKZIP utility, 160
File menu commands (Notepad), 45-46

files
    compressing, 160
    decompressing, 162-163
    downloading, 27, 36-38
        Forums, 126-127
        from Mail, 96-97
        moving files, 98-100
    exporting, 40
    retrieving from Filing Cabinet, 38-39
    sending through e-mail, 90-94
Filing Cabinet icon, 38-39
financial services, stocks
    charting performance, 138-139
    inputting, 135-136
    portfolio, 140
    quotes, 139-141
    ticker symbols, 136-138
Find icon, 21-24
Flights For dialog box, 117
folders, 38
forums
    Bacchus Wine Forum, 129
    browsing, 128-130
    downloading files, 126-127
    IBM Communications Forum, 124
    messages, 130-133
    pricing, 122
    searching, 122-125
    threads, 128
    Toolbox, 122-124

G-H

Get New Mail dialog box, 84
Get New Mail icon, 83
GIF files, 93
Go dialog box, 21
Go icon, 20-21

Hayes-compatible modems, 4
help
    downloading help information, 34-35
    WinCIM
        context-sensitive help, 30-32
        customer service, 35
        online help, 33-35
Help menu commands, Search for Help on, 31

I

IBM Communications Forum, 124
internal modems, 1
Internet
   addresses, 105
   Internet forum, 105-106
   receiving messages, 104-105
   sending messages, 102-103
itineraries (travel), 119-120

J-L

JPEG files, 93
jumper switches, 155-156

Leave icon, 59

M

Magazine Database Plus (CIM), 62-67
Mail, 75-76
   automating, 87-88
   copying, 87
   downloading files, 96-97
      moving files, 98-100
   files, sending, 90-94
   filing messages, 86-87
   Internet
      addresses, 105
      receiving messages, 104-105
      sending messages, 102-103
   Out-Basket, 77, 81-82
   pasting, 87
   reading messages offline, 85-86
   receiving messages, 84-85
   sending messages, 81-82
   writing messages
      entering text, 79
      Message Options dialog box, 80
      recipients, 77-79
      subject, 79
Mail menu commands
   Create Forum Message, 131
   Create Mail, 77
   Send File, 90
   Send/Receive All Mail, 87
Member Directory, 70-71
Members Service dialog box, 16

menu bar (WinCIM), 14-15
menus (Windows), 150-151
Message Options dialog box, 80
messages
   entering text, 79
   filing, 86-87
   forums, 130-133
   Internet
      receiving, 104-105
      sending, 102-103
   reading offline, 85-86
   receiving, 84-85
   recipients, 77-79
   sending, 81
   subject, 79
modems, 1
   baud rates, 5
      changing, 157
      customizing, 143
   communications ports, 9
   Hayes-compatible modems, 4
   system requirements, 3-5
   troubleshooting
      call waiting, 156-157
      COM ports, 155
      disconnect problems, 157
      jumper switches, 155-156
mouse, 149-150
moving downloaded files, 98-100

N-O

Names/Addresses/Phone Directories menu, 57
news stories, 47-50
News/Weather/Sports window, 50-51
Notepad, 40-41
   editing documents, 43-44
   opening documents, 41-43
   printing, 45-46
   Undo command (Edit menu), 44-45
   word wrap, 42-43

online help (WinCIM), 33-34
opening Notepad documents, 41-43
Out-Basket (Mail), 77, 81-82

Index   167

P

passwords, 9-11
pasting e-mail, 87
Phone*File, 57-60
PKZIP utility, 124-125, 160-163
Preferences command (Special menu), 144-146
Premium Services window, 28-29
pricing, 4
    alternative pricing plan, 159
    determining cost, 25-27
    forums, 122
    premium services, 27
    pricing codes, 159
    sending files through e-mail, 90
    standard pricing plan, 158
    stock charts, 138
Print command (Notepad File menu), 46
Print Setup command (Notepad File menu), 45
printing Notepad documents, 45-46
publications, 62-67
Published Fares For dialog box, 117

Q

QuickSearch (Electronic Mall), 112-113
quotes (stocks), 139-141
Quotes icon, 135

R

rates, 25-27
reading e-mail messages offline, 85-86
receiving e-mail messages, 84-85
    Internet, 104-105
Recipient List dialog box, 77
reference materials, 54-55
    encyclopedia, 55-57
    Phone*File, 57-60
Reply to Forum Message dialog box, 130
replying to forum messages, 130-131
retrieving files from Filing Cabinet, 38-39

Ribbon (WinCIM), 15
    Address Book icon, 69
    Browse icon, 55
    Disconnect icon, 18
    Exit icon, 18
    Favorite Places icon, 23-24
    Filing Cabinet icon, 38
    Find icon, 21-24
    Get New Mail icon, 83
    Go icon, 20-21
    Leave icon, 59
    Mail icon, 76
    Out-Basket icon, 81-82
    Quotes icon, 135
    Weather icon, 52

S

Search dialog box, 32
Search for Files dialog box, 125
Search for Help on command (Help menu), 31
Search Results dialog box, 22
searching
    forums, 122, 124-125
    Magazine Database Plus (CIM), 64-67
    Member Directory, 70-71
    Phone*File, 57-60
    ticker symbols, 136-138
Select Airport dialog box, 116
Send File command (Mail menu), 90
Send/Receive All Mail command (Mail menu), 87
sending e-mail messages, 81-82
    Internet, 102-103
Services window, 15
Session Settings command (Special menu), 142
shopping, 107-113
Sign Up command (Signup menu), 6
signing up, 6-9
Signup - Account Information dialog box, 10
Signup - Billing/Country dialog box, 6
Signup menu commands, Sign Up, 6
sizing windows, 153
Special menu commands
    Preferences, 144-146
    Session Settings, 142

standard pricing plan, 4, 158
starting
    applications (Windows), 150
    EAASY SABRE, 114-117
    WinCIM, 12-13
    Windows, 147
stocks
    charting performance, 138-139
    inputting, 135-136
    portfolio, 140
    quotes, 139-141
    ticker symbols, 136-138
Subject Guide dialog box, 64
switching between windows, 153
Sysops, 121
system requirements, 3-5

T

text files, 93
threads (forums), 128
ticker symbols (stocks), 136-138
Toolbox (forums), 122-124
travel, EAASY SABRE (CIM), 114-117
    fares, 117-118
    itineraries, 119-120
troubleshooting, 155-157

U-V

Undo command (Notepad Edit menu), 44-45
unzipping files, 162-163
user ID numbers, 9-11
    see also Address Book

viewing Magazine Database Plus (CIM), 66-67

W-Z

Weather icon, 52
weather maps, 51-53
weather reports, 50-51
WinCIM, 2-3
    connecting to CompuServe, 16-17
    customizing
        Preferences command (Special menu), 144-146
        Session Settings command (Special menu), 142
    desktop, 13-15
    disconnecting from CompuServe, 17-18
    exiting, 17-18
    help
        context-sensitive help, 30-32
        customer service, 35
        downloading help information, 34-35
        online help, 33-34
    starting, 12-13
    system requirements, 3-5
Windows
    applications, starting, 150
    dialog boxes, 151-153
    menus, 150-151
    mouse, 149-150
    screen components, 148-149
    starting, 147
windows
    closing, 50
    News/Weather/Sports, 50-51
    Premium Services, 28-29
    Services, 15
    sizing, 153
    switching between, 153
Windows menu commands, Close All, 50
word wrap (Notepad), 42-43
Word Wrap command (Word Wrap Edit menu), 43
writing e-mail messages, 77-80